It is with a great level of satisfaction that I write a few lines about the publication of Cameira Associados, "Portuguese Business Law".

The cover of a myriad of complex issues in fourteen concise user-friendly chapters, speaks volumes for the abilities of Maria Antónia Cameira and her team of associates.

I believe that this book answers the many queries that substantial numbers of non-Portuguese citizens have about Portugal's legal and fiscal systems.

Manuel de Teves Costa
Vice-Chairman
CPE, Portuguese Studies Group

Often corporations wishing to invest in a country of which they know very little, feel it necessary to pay more attention to the analysis of the economic and financial situation than to the country's legal environment. A similar situation can arise for companies, which trade with such countries.

As part of the European Union, Portugal must face up to the serious consequences of globalisation. However the legal environment is essential and, if it is not analysed with care, can create severe difficulties.

This confirms the vital role played by lawyers in international investments. As the President of the Portuguese Bar Association (and Law Society, as we have only one professional body) I am pleased to congratulate my colleague Maria Antónia Cameira on a book, which will make a very important contribution to this subject. She knows the relevant aspects of the United Kingdom and the Portuguese legal systems very well. She has also been able to clarify the relevant information for any potential investor or company with business relations in Portugal. In so doing she has shown how lawyers can be of help to businessmen. She deserves my congratulations on behalf of the Profession.

José Miguel Júdice
President of the Portuguese Bar Association

Cameira & Associados and PACSA (Henriques da Silva, Paes de Almeida, Corrêa de Sampaio & Associados) have recently joined forces, enhancing the "depth and breadth" in their practice teams.

The synthesis resulted in a new legal group with cutting-edge financial and corporate capabilities and commitment to excellence. The group comprises more than a hundred professionals supporting the firm's international expansion.

Our M&A ,Corporate Finance, Tax and Dispute Resolution specialists bring together an unrivalled experience in cross border transactions that drive the Portuguese and international markets.

The new legal group will have offices in Lisbon and Oporto, London, S. Paulo, and Rio de Janeiro.

Pedro Paes de Almeida
Managing Partner of PACSA

Paperback ISBN 1904312179

Published in the UK by MX Publishing

10 Kingfisher Close, Stanstead Abbotts, Hertfordshire, SG12 8LQ

Portuguese

Business Law

PACSA

Lisbon/Address: Av. da Liberdade, n.º 144, 7º Dto., 1250-146 Lisbon
Telephone: 00351-21-3241600
Facsimile: 00351-21-3241616

London/Address:
Elan House, 5-11, Fetter Lane, London EC4A 1QD, England
Telephone: 0044-207-4471200
Facsimile: 0044-207-3532468

TABLE OF CONTENTS
PORTUGUESE BUSINESS LAW 2004

15

16

BANKING
CHAPTER 1

1.1. Introduction

After the enactment of legislation in 1984, that allowed private banks and insurance companies to be organised, Portugal saw the re-emergence of some of the pre-revolutionary family groups in its economic landscape, particularly in the financial sector.

Banks and other financial services have benefited from this favourable environment, expanding through reorganization. All public banks, therefore, have been privatized, except for the Caixa Geral de Depósitos Group. As a consequence of these privatizations, acquisitions, mergers and profound internal restructuring, on the one hand, and several international strategic alliances, on the other, modern financial groups have emerged. These groups were capable of product and process innovation (for example, the Portuguese ATM network) and organizing their presence in international financial markets (through the acquisition of financial institutions - recently in Spain and Brazil - or the establishment of branches in foreign countries, mainly in the investment banking sector, frequently as joint ventures). Under these conditions, the Portuguese banking sector has been preparing for an active role in the European financial system, driven by the euro.

1.2. Legal Framework for the Portuguese Banking Sector

The Portuguese banking sector has been subject to profound structural transformation, by both national and European legislation, which has resulted in a revolution in its regulatory system and institutional framework.

1.2.1. European Union Legal Framework

The key European Union provisions regarding the legal framework for the Banking Sector are:

(i) Council Directive 93/6/EEC of 15th March 1993 on the capital adequacy of Investment Firms and credit institutions, as amended by Directive 98/31/EC of the European Parliament and of the Council of 22nd June 1998;

(ii) Council Directive 93/22/EEC of 10th May 1993 on investment services in the securities field;

(iii) Directive 94/19/EC of the European Parliament and of the Council of 30th May 1994 on deposit-guarantee schemes;

(iv) Directive 97/9/EC of the European Parliament and of the Council of 3rd March 1997, on investor-compensation schemes;

(v) Directive 2000/12/EC of the European Parliament and of the Council of 20th March 2000 relating to the establishment and operation of credit institutions, as amended by Directive 2000/28/EC of 18th March 2000;

(vi) Directive 2000/46/EC of the European Parliament and of the Council of 18th September 2000 on the establishment, operation and prudential supervision of the business of electronic money institutions;

(vii) Directive 2001/24/EC of the European Parliament and of the Council of 4th April 2001 on the reorganisation and winding up of credit institutions;

(viii) Regulation (EC) no. 2560/2001 of the European Parliament and of the Council of 19th December 2001 on cross-border payments in euro;

(ix) Directive 2002/87/EC of the European Parliament and of the Council of 16th December 2002 on the supplementary supervision of credit institutions, insurance companies and Investment Firms in a financial conglomerate and amending Council Directives 73/239/EEC, 79/267/EEC, 92/49/EEC, 92/96/EEC, 93/6/EEC and 93/22/EEC, and Directives 98/78/EC and 2000/12/EC of the European Parliament and of the Council;

(x) 2004/5/EC: Commission Decision of 5th November 2003 establishing the Committee of European Banking Supervisors;

(xi) 2004/10/EC: Commission Decision of 5th November 2003 establishing the European Banking Committee.

1.2.2. Portuguese Legal Framework

The key Portuguese provisions governing Portuguese banking activities are the following:

(i) Decree-Law 298/92 of 31st December 1992, as amended by Decree-Laws 246/95 of 14th September 1995, 232/96 of 5th December 1995, 222/99 of 2nd June 1999 (which also created an investor-compensation scheme), 250/2000 of 13th October 2000, 285/2001 of 3rd November 2001, 201/2002 of 26th September and 319/2002 of 28th December introduced the legal framework for the activities of credit institutions and finance companies (*regime geral das instituições de crédito e sociedades financeiras*) as well as the provision of investment services, since it also implemented Council Directive 93/22/EEC of 10th May 1993 (the so-called investment services directive);

(ii) Decree-Law 333/2001 of 24th December 2001, implementing Directive 98/31/EC of the European Parliament and of the Council of 22nd June 1998, amending Council Directive 93/6/EEC of 15th March 1993 on the capital adequacy of Investment Firms and credit institutions;

(iii) Decree-Law 42/2002 of 2nd March 2002, implementing Directives 2000/28/EC and 2000/46/EC of the European Parliament and of the Council, of 20th March 2000 and of 18th September 2002, respectively, and regulating the establishment, operation and prudential supervision of the business of electronic money institutions;

(iv) The Portuguese Securities Code, as approved by Decree-Law 468/99 of 13th November 1999, with subsequent amendments, with regard to the establishment and operation of financial activities within the Portuguese capital markets, discussed in the chapter "Capital Markets" of this Guide.

1.3. Entities Operating in the Portuguese Banking Sector

According to the Portuguese legal framework for the activities of credit institutions and financial entities, which is essentially embodied in Decree-Law 298/92 of 31st December 1992, there are three types of entities operating in the Portuguese financial system: credit institutions, financial companies and investment firms.

Decree-Laws 186/2002 of 21st August 2002, 201/2002 of 26th September 2002 and 319/2002 of 28th September 2002 have brought changes to the type of institutions included in each of these groups.

1.3.1. Credit Institutions

Credit institutions are defined as the entities whose activities involve receiving deposits or other repayable funds from the public and investing them, granting credit or issuing means of payment in the form of electronic money.

1.3.1.1. Types of Credit Institutions

The following are considered legally admissible types of credit institutions:

i) Banks;

ii) Savings banks;

iii) The Agricultural Central Credit Bank;

iv) Investment companies;

v) Leasing companies;

vi) Factoring companies;

vii) Credit-purchase financing companies; and

viii) Any other companies that qualify as such by law.

With the most recent amendments to the legal framework for these entities, the following new types of credit institutions have been created:

ix) Credit Financial Institutions – by Decree-Law 186/2002;

x) Mutual Guarantee Companies - by Decree-Law 201/2002;

xi) Electronic Currency Institutions – by Directive 2000/28 CE, from the Parliament and Council, of 18th September 2000.

These reforms have also eliminated the specific reference made to *Caixa Geral de Depósitos, Crédito e Previdência* (National Savings Bank) since this institution, without prejudice to the competences stipulated by law, fits the concept of bank.

1.3.1.2. Activities that may be carried out by Credit Institutions

The activities that may be carried out by banks are listed in article 4 of Decree-law 298/92, and are the following:

i) acceptance of deposits or other repayable funds;

ii) credit operations, including the granting of guarantees and other securities, financial leasing and factoring;

iii) payment operations;

iv) issuance and management of means of payment such as credit cards, travellers cheques and letters of credit;

v) trading, on the company's own account or on the accounts of customers, in money and foreign-exchange market instruments, in forward financial instruments and options, the carrying out of transactions on foreign exchange, interest rates, commodities and transferable securities;

vi) participation in the issuance and placement of securities and the provision of services related to these operations;

vii) money broking;

viii) provision of securities portfolio consultancy, safekeeping and management services;

ix) provision of management and consultancy services in relation to other portfolios;

x) provision of corporate consultancy services with regard to capital structure, industrial strategy and matters relating to mergers and acquisitions;

xi) precious metals and stones transactions;

xii) acquisition of holdings in companies;

xiii) trading in insurance policies;

xiv) credit reference services;

xv) safe custody services;

xvi) letting of movable assets other than those returned by the lessee within a leasing agreement;

xvii) providing investment services referred to in article 199-A, when not included in the abovementioned activities;

xviii) any other related activities not forbidden by law.

1.3.1.3. Requirements for the Authorisation of Credit Institutions in Portugal

Credit institutions can only operate under prior authorisation granted on a case-by-case basis by the supervisory body for the financial system, the *Banco de Portugal* (hereinafter the *Bank of Portugal*), which must notify the Commission of the European Community of each license it grants.

Applications must be accompanied by:

(i) A description of the type of institution to be incorporated and a draft of its memorandum and Articles of Association;

ii) A programme of the operations to be carried out, full information on geographical location, internal organisation, material, technical and human resources to be used and prospective accounts for each of the first three business years;

iii) An indication of the identities of the founding shareholders, including information on the size of each one's shareholding;

iv) A reasoned memorandum on the adequacy of the proposed share capital structure with regard to the institution's stability;

v) A statement that the share capital shall be deposited in a bank upon the incorporation of the institution;

vi) Full information on each of the corporate shareholders who hold qualifying shareholding in the institution, including an indication of existing qualifying holdings in each of the shareholder's own share capital as well as of qualifying holdings in other companies held by each of the same shareholders. A shareholder is deemed to have a qualifying holding whenever he is able to exercise a significant influence in the management of the credit institution. That influence is presumed to exist whenever the shareholder holds at least 10 % of the share capital or voting rights. However, this presumption can be refuted if the holding is equal or inferior to 5 % of the share capital or of the voting rights.

The *Bank of Portugal* may refuse the authorisation if these requirements are not complied with or if it finds that the institution does not have the technical or financial means to fulfil the proposed corporate objective.

Additionally, for the registration of credit institutions with their head offices in Portugal, the following general requirements must be complied with:
- The credit institution's corporate name and objective, date of incorporation, location of head office, share capital (including paid-up share capital), indication of qualifying shareholders, corporate structure, including identification of corporate body members, delegation of management powers and shareholder's agreements, date of commencement of activities, specification of existing branches and/or agencies and identification of the managers of those located abroad.

1.3.1.4. Authorisation of a Subsidiary of a Credit Institution Already Authorised by Another European Union Member State

The *Bank of Portugal* can only authorise the incorporation and operation of a credit institution, which is a subsidiary of a credit institution already authorised by the competent authorities of another European Union Member State, or a subsidiary of the parent company of such an institution, upon prior consultation with the supervisory authority of the Member State in question. This requirement also applies where the institution to be incorporated is controlled by the same individuals or entities that control a credit institution authorised by another EU Member State.

Additionally, for the registration of credit institutions with their head offices in other European Union Member States the following general requirements must be complied with:
- corporate name, location of head office, date on which the may commence their activities in Portugal, specification of branches, agencies or representations offices in Portugal as well as identification of their respective managers and specification of the business covered by the authorisation granted in their home country and of the business envisaged in Portugal.

1.3.1.5. Specific Regulations for Subsidiaries of Credit Institutions with Head Offices in Non-European Union Countries

The provisions applicable to subsidiaries of credit institutions authorised by the competent authorities of EU countries also apply, with the appropriate adjustments, to the authorisation of credit institutions with their head offices in Portugal, where:

a) Such institutions are subsidiaries of credit institutions, which have their head offices in non-EU countries; or

b) They are controlled, or the majority of their share capital or corresponding voting rights are held by, individuals from a non-EU country or by legal entities, which have their head offices in non-EU countries.

However, such an authorisation shall be granted on a case-by-case basis by the Minister of Finance, in the form of an executive order, which may delegate such power to the *Bank of Portugal*. The application for authorisation must be filed with the *Bank of Portugal*, which may request additional information and conduct such enquiries as may be deemed necessary.

The abovementioned authorisation shall only be granted provided that none of the grounds for refusal of the authorisation mentioned above are identified and that the creation of the credit institution contributes to an improvement in the efficiency of the national banking system or has a significant effect on the internationalisation of the Portuguese economy, in line with Portuguese economic and financial policies.

Under certain circumstances, the *Bank of Portugal* may be required to impose restrictions on the licences granted to the entities mentioned above or suspend the procedures for evaluating pending requests for authorisation, as specified by the Commission of the European Communities in a decision taken under article 23(4) of Directive 2000/12/EC.

General requirements, as seen with subsidiaries of credit institutions already authorised in another EU Member State are also applicable here.

1.3.1.6. Requirements for the Establishment of Branches

1.3.1.6.1. Of a Portuguese Credit Institution in a European Union Member State

A credit institution with its head office in Portugal, which desires to set up a branch within the territory of another EU Member State shall notify the *Bank of Portugal* of this intention in advance, providing the following information:

- Indication of the country in which the proposed branch is to be established and of the address of that branch;
- Identification of branch managers;
- The programme of operations for the proposed branch, setting out the type of business envisaged and its structural organisation.

26

The day-to-day management of such a branch must be entrusted to at least two managers who are subject to all the requirements imposed on the members of the board of directors of credit institutions, as described below.

1.3.1.6.2. Of a Portuguese Credit Institution in Non-European Union Countries
A credit institution with its head office in Portugal, which desires to establish a branch in a non-European Union country must comply with the requirements for establishment of a branch within EU territory as described above with regard to the prior notification to the *Bank of Portugal*.

The *Bank of Portugal* may refuse the necessary authorisation for the establishment of the branch should it have reasonable doubt as regards the organisational or financial adequacy of the business envisaged by the proposed branch.

The branch may not carry out business, which the parent institution is not allowed to carry out in Portugal or that falls outside the scope of the programme of operations presented to the *Bank of Portugal*.

1.3.1.6.3. Of a Credit Institution Authorised by Another European Union Member State
A credit institution authorised by another EU Member State can only establish a branch within Portugal where the *Bank of Portugal* was previously notified of the said institution's intention by the supervisory authority of its home Member State. The notification must include:
- A programme of operations setting out the business envisaged by, and the structural organisation of, the branch, as well as certification that those activities are covered by the credit institution's authorisation;
- Identification of branch managers;
- Indication of the credit institution's solvency ratio;
- Detailed memorandum on the deposit-guarantee and investor-compensation schemes in which the credit institution participates, applying to the branch's clients.

1.3.1.6.4. Of a Branch of a Credit Institution Authorised by a Non-European Union Country
A credit institution authorised by non-European country is required to apply for prior permission from the *Bank of Portugal* to establish a branch within Portugal. Such permission is granted, on a case-by-case basis, by the Minister of Finance or by the *Bank of Portugal*, under delegation of those powers.

The application for authorisation must include the information mentioned above, and also:

- Evidence of the branch's capacity to ensure the safekeeping of the funds entrusted to it, as well as of the adequacy of its technical means and financial resources in relation to the type and volume of business envisaged;
- Indication of the proposed geographical location of the branch;
- Copy of the credit institution's Articles of Association;
- A statement that the branch shall be endowed with capital of an amount equal to, or greater than, the minimum share capital required for the incorporation of a similar credit institution in Portugal.

The branch must be endowed with an amount of capital adequate for the operations envisaged, but no less than the minimum share capital required by Portuguese law for the incorporation of credit institutions of the same type in Portugal. Deposit of this capital with a credit institution prior to the registration of the branch with the *Bank of Portugal* is obligatory.

1.3.1.7. Supply of Services by a Credit Institution

1.3.1.7.1. In Other European Union Member States

Credit institutions having their head offices in Portugal, which desire to carry out the businesses listed in Annex 1 to Directive 2000/12/EC of the European Parliament and of the Council of 20th March 2000 (equivalent, in the essence, to the businesses referred to in items (i) to (x), (xiv) and (xv) of section 1.3.1.2. above) in another EU Member State by way of supply of services, i.e., without recourse to a permanent establishment in that Member State, must previously notify the *Bank of Portugal* of such an intention, specifying the business envisaged.

The provision of such services must comply with the regulations applying to external and foreign exchange transactions.

1.3.1.7.2. In Portugal

A credit institution authorised by another European Union Member State to carry out activities listed in Annex I to Directive 2000/12/EC (see section 1.3.1.4.3. above) is allowed to conduct such business within Portugal by way of the supply of services, i.e., without recourse to a permanent establishment in the said territory.

Prior to the commencement of the credit institutions activities, the supervisory authority of the credit institution's home Member State must notify the *Bank of Portugal* of the business envisaged by the credit institution within Portugal, and certify that such activities are covered by the licence granted in the home Member State.

1.3.1.8. Representative Offices of Foreign Credit Institutions in Portugal

Credit institutions whose head offices are abroad are required to register their representative offices in the Portugal with the *Bank of Portugal* prior to the commencement of those offices' activities, without prejudice to the applicability of the relevant legislation on commercial registration. This involves the presentation of a certificate issued by the supervisory authorities of the home country, specifying the legal system governing the credit institution by referring to the applicable law. The activities of the credit institution must commence within three months of its registration.

The activities of representative offices are strictly dependent on the credit institutions, which they represent, in that they are only permitted to look after the interests of these institutions in Portugal and to provide information on the activities, which they intend to pursue.

Representative offices are forbidden to carrying out directly transactions that fall within the scope of the activities of the credit institutions, to acquire shares or holdings in any Portuguese companies or to acquire property other than that required for their establishment and operation.

1.3.2. Financial Companies

A financial institution is regarded as a company that carries out one or more of the activities listed in article 4, except accepting deposits or other repayable funds, leasing and factoring, without being a credit institution.

1.3.2.1. Types of Financial Companies

The following are considered legally admissible types of financial companies:

i) dealers;

ii) brokers;

iii) foreign-exchange or money-market intermediation companies;

iv) investment fund managing companies;

v) credit card or asset managing companies;

vi) regional development companies;

vii) venture capital companies;

viii) exchange offices; and

ix) credit securitisation fund managing companies (Decree-Law 201/2002)

The "credit securitisation fund management company", another type of financial institution, was introduced by the most recent legislation.

1.3.2.2. Scope of Activities

Financial companies can only carry out business defined by the specific laws and regulations governing their respective activities. The key legislative provisions in force applicable to finance companies are the following:

i)   Dealers and Brokers (*sociedades corretoras e sociedades financeiras de corretagem*) - Decree-Law 262/2001 of 28th September 2001;

ii)   Foreign-exchange or money-market mediating companies (*sociedades mediadoras dos mercados monetário ou de câmbios*) – Decree-Law 110/94, of 28th April 1994;

iii)   Fund management companies (*sociedades gestoras de fundos de investimento*)- Decree-Law 229-C/1988 of 4th July 1988, as amended by Decree-Law 417/91 of 26th October 1991 (investment funds); Decree-Law 276/94, of 2nd November, as amended by Decrees-Law 308/95 of 20th November 1995, 323/97 of 26th November 1997 and 323/99 of 13th August 1999 (securities investment funds) and by Decree-Law 60/2002 of 20th March 2002 (real property investments);

iv)   Credit card issuing or managing companies (*sociedades emissoras ou gestoras de cartões de crédito*) - Decree-Law 166/95 of 15th July 1995 and Notice (*aviso*) of the *Bank of Portugal* no. 4/95 of 28th July 1995;

v)   Asset management companies (*sociedades gestoras de patrimónios*) - Decree-Law 163/94 of 4th June 1994, as amended by Decree-Law 17/97 of 21st January 1997 and by Decree-Law 99/98, of 21st April 1998;

vi)   Regional development companies (*sociedades de desenvolvimento regional*) - Decree-Law 25/91, of 11th January 1991, as amended by Decree-Law 247/94, of 7th October 1994;

vii)   Venture capital companies (*sociedades de capital de risco*) – Decree-Law 433/91, of 7th November as amended by Decree-Law 175/94, of 27th June 1994 and by Decree-Law 230/98, of 22nd July 1998 and Decree-Law 58/99 of 2nd March 1999 (venture capital funds);

viii)   Currency exchange offices (*agências de câmbio*) - Decree-Law 3/94 of 11 January 1994, as amended by Decree-Law 298/95 of 18th November 1995 and by Decree-Law 53/2001 of 15th February 2001, Government Order 28/94 of 11th January 1994 and Notice (*aviso*) of the *Bank of Portugal* no. 3/2001 of 20th March 2001.

1.3.2.3. Requirements for the Authorisation of a Financial Company in Portugal

The incorporation of a financial company in Portugal requires prior authorisation given on a case-by-case basis by the *Bank of Portugal*, to which the same set of requirements and formalities for the authorisation of credit institutions also applies.

Any amendments to the Articles of Association of a financial company, including its merger, demerger and winding up, also require, previous authorisation by the *Bank of Portugal.*

Additionally, for the registration of financial companies that have head offices in Portugal, the following general requirements must be complied with:
- that they resemble one of the types of companies identified by Portuguese law;
- that they have, as their corporate objective, one or more of the activities mentioned in article 5 of Decree-Law 298/92 of 31st December 1992 or in specific legislation;
- that they have a share capital equal or greater than the minimum share capital required by law.

A part of the share capital (which must be equal to at least the minimum share capital) must be fully paid up at the time of incorporation of the financial company.

1.3.2.4. Branches of Financial Companies Subsidiaries of Credit Institutions

1.3.2.4.1. Branches of Financial Companies which are Subsidiaries of Portuguese Credit Institutions in Other EU Countries

The establishment in other EU Member States of branches of financial companies with their head offices in Portugal must comply with the requirements applicable to credit institutions desiring to establish branches in other EU Member States, described above.

(a) The said financial companies are subsidiaries of one or more credit institutions governed by Portuguese law and thereby authorised to carry out one or more of the activities listed in Annex 1 to Directive 2000/12/EC of the European Parliament and of the Council of 20th March 2000;

b) Those financial companies comply with the following requirements:
i) The parent company or companies are authorised as credit institutions in Portugal;
ii) The activities in question are actually performed within Portugal;
iii) The parent company or companies hold 90% or more of the voting rights attached to the subsidiary's share capital;

iv) The parent company or companies satisfy the requirements imposed by the *Bank of Portugal* regarding the prudent management of the subsidiary and declare, with the consent of the same Bank, that they jointly and severally guarantee the commitments entered into by the subsidiary; and

v) The subsidiary is both covered by the supervision applying to its parent company or companies and subject to independent supervision in its own right.

1.3.2.4.2. Branches of Financial Companies which are Subsidiaries of Credit Institutions whose Head Offices are in Other EU Countries

The establishment in Portugal of branches of financial companies whose head offices are in other EU Member States must comply with the requirements applying to finance companies with head offices in Portugal in respect of corporate name registration and settlement and operation of branches within Portugal, where:

(a) The said financial companies are subsidiaries of one or more credit institutions governed by the law of another EU Member State and are thereby authorised to carry out one or more of the activities listed in Annex 1 to Directive 2000/12/EC of the European Parliament and of the Council of 20th March 2000 (equivalent, in essence, to the activities referred to in items (i) to (x) and (xv) of section 1.3.1.2. above);

b) Those financial companies comply with the following requirements:

i) The parent company or companies are authorised as credit institutions in the home Member State;

ii) The activities in question are actually performed within the territory of that Member State;

iii) The parent company or companies hold 90% or more of the voting rights attached to the subsidiary's share capital;

iv) The parent company or companies satisfy the requirements imposed by the home Member State's Central Bank regarding the prudent management of the subsidiary and declare, with the consent of the same Bank, that they jointly and severally guarantee the commitments entered into by the subsidiary;

v) The subsidiary is both covered by the supervision applying to its parent company or companies and subject to independent supervision in its own right.

1.3.2.5. Other Branches of Financial Companies which are not Subsidiaries of Credit Institutions

1.3.2.5.1. With Head Office in Portugal

Financial companies with their head offices in Portugal, which do not comply with the requirements, set out above, and which intend to establish branches outside Portugal must comply with the requirements applying to credit institutions desiring to establish branches in non-EU countries, described in this chapter.

1.3.2.5.2. With their head offices abroad

Financial companies that either have their head offices in other EU Member States but do not comply with the abovementioned requirements or have their head offices in a non-EU countries, and desire to establish a branch within Portugal, must abide by the requirements applying to the settlement of branches of credit institutions authorised by non-EU countries, described above.

The authorisation for the establishment in Portugal of the branches of the abovementioned financial companies cannot be granted in such terms as to permit the former to carry out a wider range of activities than those permitted to institutions of a similar nature whose head offices are in Portugal.

1.3.2.6. Supply of Services by a Financial Company

1.3.2.6.1. By a Portuguese Financial Company in other European Union Member States

Financial companies with their head offices in Portugal which comply with the requirements described in section 1.3.2.4.1. above, and which desire to provide services in another European Union Member State without recourse to a permanent establishment therein, are required to notify the *Bank of Portugal* of their intention. Such notification must be accompanied by documentary evidence of the compliance with the abovementioned requirements.

1.3.2.6.2. By Financial Companies with Head Offices in Other EU Countries

Finance companies with head offices in other EU Member States, which comply with the requirements described in section 1.3.2.4.2. above, and which desire to provide services in Portugal without recourse to a permanent establishment therein, are required to notify the *Bank of Portugal* of their intention. Such notification must be accompanied by a certificate issued by the supervisory authorities of the home Member State proving compliance with the requirements referred to in section above.

1.3.2.7. Establishment of Representative Offices of Financial Companies

The establishment and operation in Portugal of representative offices of financial institutions whose head offices abroad must comply with the requirements applying to the establishment of representative offices of credit institutions, described above.

1.3.3. Investment Firms

Decree-Law 232/96 of 5th December 1996, which amended Decree-Law 298/92, introduced some definitions concerning investment services and companies.

Investment companies are those companies whose regular activities include providing professional investment services to third parties. They are, subject to the requirements concerning the use of their own funds of the Council Directive 93/6/EEC of 15th March 1993, as amended by European Parliament and Council Directive 98/31/EC of 22nd of June 1998, except for credit institutions and individuals.

1.3.3.1. Investment Services

According to Decree-Law 298/92, the services provided by these companies are the following:

i) Receipt and execution, of orders relating to any of the financial instruments listed in Section B of Directive 93/22/CEE of 10th May 1993, on behalf of investors:

- securities;
- units in collective investment undertaking;
- money-market instruments;
- financial-futures contracts;
- forward interest-rate agreements (FRAs);
- interest-rate, currency and equity swaps;
- options to acquire or dispose of any of the instruments falling within section B of the annex to Directive 93/22/CEE;

ii) execution of the abovementioned orders;

iii) dealing, on their own account, in any of the abovementioned instruments;

iv) managing investment portfolios within the scope of the mandate given by the investors, on a discretionary and client-by-client basis, whenever those portfolios include any of the abovementioned instruments; and

v) placing, with or without underwriting, any of the said financial instruments;

1.3.3.2. Legal Framework

The provisions of Decree-Law 298/92 that apply to financial institutions also apply to Investment Firms.

1.4. Prudential Rules

1.4.1. Common Rule

Credit institutions must invest their available funds in such a way as to ensure appropriate levels of liquidity and solvency at all times.

1.4.2. Minimum Share Capital

The Minister of Finance establishes, by government order, the minimum share capital of Credit institutions, which is also required where the institution is incorporated through a merger or demerger.

1.4.3. Own Funds and Statutory Reserves

The *Bank of Portugal* sets out the assets that may comprise the funds of credit institutions, which must not be inferior to the amount of the share capital. If funds of credit institutions become inferior to their share capital, the *Bank of Portugal* can give the institution a limited deadline to top up its funds.

Furthermore, a minimum of 10% of the net profits obtained in each fiscal year must be allocated to a statutory reserve up to a limit equal to the amount of the share capital, or to the sum of the existing voluntary reserves and previous years results, if this amount is superior.

1.5. Supervision

The Ministry of Finance oversees monetary, financial and foreign exchange markets. It co-ordinates the activities of market operators according to the Government's economic and social policy, pursuant to Decree-Law 298/92.

Whenever a disturbance that can seriously jeopardize the domestic economy arises in these markets, the Government, with the advice of the *Bank of Portugal*, may require that appropriate action be taken, namely the temporary suspension of certain markets or types of transactions, or even the temporary closure of credit institutions.

The Bank of Portugal, as the supervisory authority is responsible for guiding and controlling the monetary and exchange markets, as well as regulating, controlling and promoting the proper functioning of payment schemes in the context of its participation in the European System of Central Banks. It is also responsible for compiling statistics concerning monetary, financial and foreign exchange matters as well as the balance of payments, in the context of cooperation with the European Central Bank.

The supervision of credit institutions, including that of their activities abroad, is the responsibility of the *Bank of Portugal*. However, these powers may not compromise the competence of the Stock Market Supervisory Authority (*Comissão de Mercados de Valores Mobiliários*) or the Insurance Supervisory Authority (*Instituto de Seguros de Portugal*).

In the performance of its supervisory duties, the *Bank of Portugal* has the following responsibilities:
i) monitoring the activity of credit institutions;
ii) overseeing compliance by credit institutions of regulations concerning their activities;
ii) issuing recommendations in order to resolve any irregularities detected;
iv) taking extraordinary reorganisation measures; and
v) imposing penalties on infractions.

The *Bank of Portugal* may require that special audits be conducted by an independent entity, which it designates for that specific purpose, at the expense of the audited institution.

1.6. Deposit Guarantee Fund (*"Fundo de Garantia de Depósitos"*)
According to Decree-Law 298/92 of 31st December 1992 and Council Directive 94/19/CE, of 30th May 1994, the Deposit Guarantee Fund is a legal body governed by public law, with administrative and financial autonomy and with its head offices in Lisbon, in the premises of the *Bank of Portugal*, the purpose of which is to ensure depositor protection by guaranteeing the repayment of deposits with participating credit institutions.

Participation in the scheme is compulsory for the following institutions listed in article 156/1:
- Credit institutions whose head offices are in Portugal and are authorised to take deposits there; and
- Credit institutions with their head offices in non-EU Member States in relation to deposits taken by their branches in Portugal, unless those deposits are covered by a guarantee scheme established

by the *Bank of Portugal,* which is equivalent to the scheme instituted by the *Fundo de Garantia de Depósitos*, without prejudice to any existing bilateral agreement on the subject.

1.7. Corporate Governance for Banking

1.7.1. Introduction

In Portugal there are special corporate governance requirements for banks, which are chiefly covered by Decree-Law 298/92, of 31st December, last amended by Decree-Law 201/2002, of 26th September and Decree-Law 319/2002, of 28th December, the General Regime of Credit Institutions and Financial Companies ("*Regime Geral das Instituições de Crédito e Sociedades Financeiras*").

The Portuguese Banking Supervisory Authority (The *Bank of Portugal*) is the authority that supervises the banks' compliance with corporate governance requirements. However, the Stock Market Supervisory Authority ("CMVM") also has an important supervisory role with reference to listed credit institutions.

According to Law n. 5/98, of 31st January 1998, as amended by Decree-Law 118/2001, of 17th April 2001 (The *Bank of Portugal* Organic Law), the Bank of Portugal shall be responsible for the supervision of credit institutions, financial companies and other entities legally subject to its authority, by issuing directives, namely Notices (*Avisos*), published in the Official Gazette, Regulatory instruments (*Instruções*), or published in Regulation and Information Bulletin of the *Bank of Portugal* (*Boletim de Normas e Informações do Banco de Portugal*- BNBP), or via the Manual of Instructions (set of Regulatory instruments in force) and through Circular Letters (non-regulatory guidelines disclosed through BNBP) to guide their performance and to ensure that credit risks can be centrally monitored. For that purpose, the *Bank of Portugal* may require any information deemed necessary for compliance with such provisions from any public or private body or in order to satisfy its remit.

Credit institutions can only be incorporated as joint stock companies ("anónima" companies). Therefore and according to the Portuguese Companies Code, two models of governance for "anónima" companies can be adopted, namely a unitary management structure or a two-tier structure.

Basel Committee working papers on Banking Supervision namely, *Principles for the management of interest rate risk* (September 1997), *Enhancing Corporate Governance for Banking*

Organisations (September1998), *Enhancing bank transparency* (September 1998) and *Principles for the management of credit risk* (a consultative document in July 1999), set out important guidelines on corporate governance, which largely inspired Portuguese corporate governance provisions for credit institutions.

The Portuguese legal framework for the corporate governance of banks and other credit institutions draws extensively on the guidelines set out by the abovementioned committee, defining rules and regulations for the development of banking for boards and senior management and describing sound corporate governance practices.

Compliance with the above-mentioned frameworks allows for the efficient operation and supervision of credit institutions' organisational structures.

Contrary to sound corporate governance it is worth mentioning that the statutes of at least, two important credit institutions permit voting caps.

1.7.2. Basel Committee Recommendations

The abovementioned rules cover important corporate governance matters involving banking organisations, following the most recent trends in European legislation, namely Directive 2000/12/EC, of 20th March 2000 and the Basel Committee recommendations.

1.7.2.1. Establishing Strategic Objectives

When applying for authorisation to operate in the Portuguese market, credit institutions are legally bound to submit a set of reports and documents that clearly set out corporate strategic objectives, as well as plans for their implementation. In particular, they must submit a full and complete programme of operations, as well as a detailed description of the structure that they propose to adopt, in order to implement such a programme and a set of prospective accounts for each of the three business years. A well-founded report on the adequacy of the proposed share capital structure for the institution's stability must also be submitted.

If the *Bank of Portugal* finds that the institution does not have the technical or financial means to fulfil the proposed corporate objective, or if the institution has not complied with the abovementioned requirements, it will not authorise that institution to operate in the Portuguese banking market.

Corporate best-practice is underpinned by several legal provisions enshrined in the General Regime of Credit Institutions and Financial Companies and by credit institutions' internal regulations and codes of conduct.

These provisions contain fundamental rules of conduct for directors and employees of credit institutions in their relationships with clients, promoting diligence, neutrality, loyalty and respect of the latter's interests. They also deal with duties of disclosure in the provision of banking services.

Conflicts of interests are also addressed in these provisions, which prohibit direct or indirect loans to board members of credit institutions, as well as other forms of preferential lending to interested parties. They also expressly prohibit the intervention of these board members in any transaction where they may have any direct or indirect interests.

These provisions also regulate the granting of loans to holders of qualifying shareholdings. Loans to a single qualifying shareholder may not exceed 10 % of the funds of the credit institution while the maximum level of lending to such shareholders in total may not exceed 30% of the institution's funds. These operations also depend on the prior approval of at least two thirds of the board of directors and a favourable report from the board of auditors of the credit institution.

The members of boards of credit institutions and their staff are bound by the duty of confidentiality regarding facts related to the institution itself and the institution's relationship with its clients.

1.7.2.2. Responsibility and Accountability

In order to set and enforce clear lines of responsibility and accountability throughout the organisation, credit institutions must provide the *Bank of Portugal* with information on their administrative organisation, the effectiveness of their internal control mechanisms and security procedures regarding their database.

Moreover, credit institutions are encouraged to issue internal codes of conduct, which are subject to assessment by CMVM. The most recent example is the professional Code of Conduct of the Portuguese Association of Banks, which is mandatory on all member credit institutions.

1.7.2.3. Structure of Board of Directors

The structuring of board of directors of credit institutions as well as the appointment of directors is subject to specific personal requirements and must fulfil certain criteria.

The members of the board must display integrity and be qualified to fulfil their duties.

The directors that intend to sit on boards of other companies must apply for prior authorisation to the *Bank of Portugal*, which can be denied if it finds that this causes conflicts of interests.

Board members must register with the *Bank of Portugal*, and comply with the above-mentioned personal requirements.

Special committees, such as a risk management committee, a compensation committee and a nomination committee may be created by the credit institution's internal regulations.

Moreover, the *Bank of Portugal* can appoint temporary directors to the board of directors of Credit institutions in specific cases, such as ineffectiveness of internal control procedures, in order to ensure a proper assessment of the net asset situation of the entity in question.

1.7.2.4. Oversight by Senior Management

Portuguese provisions of the General Regime of Credit Institutions and Financial Companies stipulate that the board of directors of credit institutions must consist of at least three members with full powers to run the business of the institution and its daily management must be entrusted to at least two board members. These provisions aim to provide for compliance with the principle, which states that key management decisions should be made by more than one person ("*four eyes principle*").

1.7.2.5. Internal and External Auditors

The internal and external qualified auditors provide an important control function. They ensure that the financial information is correct. They are also obliged to report any breaches of the provisions that govern the banking activity to the *Bank of Portugal*.

Moreover, in the exercise of its supervisory powers, the *Bank of Portugal* can request special auditing of credit institutions by independent entities.

1.7.2.6. Compensation Policies

Rules concerning the compensation policy of board members of credit institutions are mainly provided by their own internal codes of conduct.

CMVM regulation 7/2001 contains rules on the duty of disclosure of board remuneration, which oblige listed credit institutions to disclose the total amount of remuneration received on an annual basis by independent and non-independent directors and distinguish fixed from variable remuneration. The validity of such compensation practices will depend on the statutes of the company and the previous approval of the shareholders.

1.7.2.7. Transparency

Communication duties, vetting by the *Bank of Portugal* regarding the acquisition of qualifying holdings and suspension of voting rights are safeguards enshrined in the Portuguese legal framework on credit institutions. The *Bank of Portugal* plays a crucial role in this context, as the supervisory authority of the banking system. Actions that depend on pior authorisation from the *Bank of Portugal* include amendments to statutes that govern credit institutions and mergers or demergers.

The acquisition or increase in qualifying holdings must be communicated to *Bank of Portugal,* which may provisionally oppose such an operation in the following three months, if it concludes that the acquirer does not fulfil the necessary conditions to guarantee a sound and prudent management of the credit institution.

In its assessment, the *Bank of Portugal* may, in certain situations, provisionally oppose the completion of the transaction, before reaching a final decision.

Whenever an action involves an increase in a qualifying holding, so that the proportion of the voting rights, or the held share capital reaches or exceeds 5 % initially and then thresholds of 10 %, 20 %, 33 % or 50 %, or so that the credit institution becomes a subsidiary of the acquirer, the *Bank of Portugal* must also receive prior notification. Likewise, the *Bank of Portugal* must be notified whenever any acquired holdings reach a minimum of 2 % of the share capital or the voting rights of a credit institution.

The Bank of Portugal can order, at any time, the suspension of the voting rights corresponding to an acquired or increased qualifying holding, if it becomes aware of facts that may justify the conclusion that the shareholder in question will not be able to guarantee a sound and prudent management of the credit institution. The *Bank of Portugal* will also determine the extent to which the suspension will include the voting rights of the credit institution in other credit institutions, with whom it maintains a dominant relationship.

Credit institutions must also provide the *Bank of Portugal* with reports on risk assessment and compliance with the regulations on internal control mechanisms.

Credit institutions are also obliged to maintain adequate levels of liquidity and solvency and, accordingly, must keep reserves, which cannot be inferior to 10 % of the annual net profits.

The implementation of these measures regulates shareholder action and influence and promotes transparency and accountability in the management of the institution and the protection of the best principles of corporate governance.

CAPITAL MARKETS

CHAPTER 2

2.1. The Portuguese Securities Code

2.1.1. The New Portuguese Securities Code: Modernisation and Internationalisation of the Portuguese Stock Market

The new Portuguese Securities Code, as approved by Decree-Law 486/99 of 13th November 1999, as amended by Decree-Law 61/2002 of 20th March 2002, revoked and replaced the Securities Code, as approved by Decree-Law 142-A/91, of 10th April 1991, which was then considered a landmark in the regulation and development of the Stock Market in Portugal and was in force for about 10 years.

The new Securities Code was enacted in order to modernise the legal securities system, taking into account international practice and foreign legislation, following international trends to standardise laws concerning capital markets operations as a way to integrate international Stock Markets and to encourage their competitiveness.

In response to the abovementioned trends, the new Securities Code introduced rules that promote trade in securities regulated by foreign law in the Portuguese Stock Market as well as special rules applicable to prospectuses of a foreign issuers and the listing of foreign securities on the Portuguese Stock Exchange. The new Securities Code also incorporates some of the principles on takeover bids contained in the proposal for a 13th Directive on company law ("Takeover Directive") recently presented to, and rejected by, the European Parliament.

The EU is currently attempting, once more, to harmonize the takeover provisions in order to increase legal certainty and to provide for a minority shareholders protection regime.

It is claimed that the new proposal is coherent and based on the 'subsidiary' and 'proportionality' principles of the Treaty. It also includes a clear definition of "equitable price", which generally refers to the highest price paid by a bidder for the class of share concerned prior to acquiring controlling holding and introduces "squeeze out" rights, which enables a successful takeover bidder, who holds not less than 90 percent of the capital carrying voting rights of the target company, to buy out minority interests, and "sell out" rights, which enables

43

residual minority shareholders to compel a successful bidder, provided that he holds 90 percent of the company's voting capital, to buy their shares at the price of the preceding takeover bid.

The proposal has two distinct "choice" components. First, it would give Member States a choice between requiring or allowing companies to adopt the principle of board neutrality, which in essence prevents boards from frustrating takeover bids. It would also give Member States a choice between requiring or allowing companies to restrict the use of certain pre-bid defences (including dual class shares) by adopting the so-called "break through" rule, when an investor, after acquiring a certain threshold of the cash flow rights to a company, should be able to break through the company's current control structure.

Second, those companies that are given the choice to, but do not opt for the EU board neutrality and break-through rules would continue to be regulated by their Member State's non-harmonised takeover rules.

This Directive is designed to provide harmonised rules for the conduct of takeover bids throughout the EU and to provide protection for minority shareholders.
To this end the Directive includes provisions which:

- Harmonise rules relating to minority squeeze out provisions.
- Harmonise rules relating to mandatory bids (especially when a mandatory bid is triggered).
- Outlaw a range of defensive measures against hostile takeovers.
- Require that before permitted defensive measures can be put in place by the target's board, prior approval must be obtained from shareholders after the bid has been made.
- Require permitted defensive measures to be approved by shareholders of the company at least every two years.
- Require that any permitted defensive mechanisms or agreements be disclosed publicly.

The compromise legislation is a striking example of Member State governments having learnt from the 2001 Parliament defeat on the previous draft takeover Directive.

The European Council has agreed to legislation that provides a genuine choice to Member States and shareholders and will open a new path for EU corporate law reforms. It remains to be seen whether these, and other concerns, will be addressed by the European Parliament.

This chapter focuses on the most relevant features of the new Portuguese Securities Code, with regard to capital market operations. The Portuguese Stock Market in general and the derivatives market in particular are also considered below.

2.2. Legal Framework

2.2.1. European Legal Framework

The new Securities Code transposed the following Community Directives relating to securities and capital markets regulations:

i) Council Directive 79/279/EEC of 5th March 1979, as amended by Council Directives 80/390/EEC of 27th March 1980, 82/148/EEC of 3rd March 1982, 87/345/EEC of 22nd June 1987, 90/211/EEC of 23rd April 1990, and 94/18/CE of 30th May 1994, co-ordinating the conditions for the admission of securities to official quotation on a Stock Exchange, repealed by Directive 2001/34/EC of 28th May 2001 of the Council and of the European Parliament, on the admission of securities to official Stock Exchange listing and on information to be published on those securities;

ii) Council Directive 82/121/CEE of 15th February 1982, repealed by Directive 2001/34/EC, on information to be published on a regular basis by companies the shares of which have been admitted to official Stock-Exchange listing;

iii) Council Directive 88/627/EEC of 12th December 1988, on the information to be published when a major holding in a listed company is acquired or disposed of, also repealed by Directive 2001/34/EC;

iv) Council Directive 89/298/CEE of 17th April 1989, coordinating the requirements for the drawing-up, scrutiny and distribution of the prospectus to be published when transferable securities are offered to the public;

v) Council Directive 89/592/CEE of 13th November 1989, coordinating regulations on insider dealing;

vi) Council Directive 93/22/EC of 10th May 1993, relating to securities investment services, as amended by European Parliament and Council Directives 95/26/EC of 29th June 1995, 97/9/EC

45

of 3rd March 1997 and 2000/64/EC of 7th November 2000, to the extent not included in the General Regime of Financial Institutions and Financial Companies, as approved by Decree-Law 232/96 of 5th December 1996, as amended;

vii)Directive 95/26/CE of the Council and European Parliament, of 29th June 1995, reinforcing supervision, also known as the post-BCCI Directive;

viii) Directive 98/26/CE of the Council and of the European Parliament, of 19th May 1998, on Settlement Finality in Payment and Securities Settlement Systems.

ix) 2001/527/EC: Commission Decision of 6th June 2001 establishing the Committee of European Securities Regulators.

x) 2001/528/EC: Commission Decision of 6th June 2001 establishing the European Securities Committee.

xi) Directive 2002/87/EC of the European Parliament and of the Council of 16th December 2002 on the supplementary supervision of credit institutions, insurance undertakings and investments companies in a financial conglomerate.

xii) Directive 2003/6/EC of the European Parliament and of the Council of 28th January 2003 on insider dealing and market manipulation (market abuse).

2.2.2. Portuguese Legal Framework

The new Securities Code enshrined the principle of Codification, according to which the Securities Code should only retain and harmonise the rules applicable to the most relevant aspects of the capital markets. Other aspects are kept outside the Code and regulated in separate legislation, such as:

i) The Legal Framework of the Stock Market Supervisory Authority (the *Comissão do Mercado de Valores Mobiliários*), as approved by Decree-Law 473/99 of 8th November 1999 amended by Decree-Law 232/00 of 25th September 2000.

ii) Decrees-Law 394/99(as amended by Decree-law 8-D/02 of 15th January 2002) and 395/99 of 13th October 1999, on the legal framework applying to managing entities of the regulated and non-regulated Stock Markets and to entities, which render services related to the management of these markets,

iii) Those relating to rating companies (*sociedades de notação de risco*), auditors, and the registration of book-entry securities, among others.

In addition, Decree-Law 221/2000 of 9th September 2000 transposed into the Portuguese legal system only the provisions of Council and European Parliament Directive 98/26/CE, of 9th May 1998 concerning financial settlement finality in financial settlement systems, namely in the case of the bankruptcy or similar financial difficulties of any of its participants, since the Securities Code itself transposed the said Directives provisions on the settlement finality of securities within settlement systems.

2.3. Main Features of the New Securities Code

The most relevant features of the new Portuguese Securities Code, with regard to capital markets operations, are briefly described below.

2.3.1. Public Offers

The new Securities Code requires for most securities transactions, the launching of a "public offer", which is defined as an offer of securities, directed in whole or in part, to undefined recipients (the uncertainty of the recipient is not prejudiced by the fact that the offer takes place through a series of standard communications, even if addressed to individually identified addressees). The Code also considers as a public offer any offer addressed to all the shareholders of a public company, even if the respective company's share capital is represented by nominative shares. Any offer which is, in whole or in part, preceded or accompanied by a prospectus or an invitation for investment, to unspecified recipients or promotional material and any offer addressed to more than 200 people will be subject to public offer regulations stipulated in the Securities Code.

2.3.1.1. Mandatory Intermediation

Public offers for securities must take place through a financial broker, who shall offer at least the following services:

i) Assistance and placement, in public offers for distribution of securities;

ii) Assistance, from the date of the preliminary announcement and receipt of the declarations of acceptance, in takeover bids.

The offeror may execute these duties by himself where he is duly authorised as a financial broker.

2.3.1.2. Prior Registration

All public offers are subject to prior registration with the *Comissão do Mercado de Valores Mobiliários* (Stock Market Supervisory Authority - CMVM) and the request for registration must be accompanied by the following documents (unless the CMVM is already in possession of an updated version thereof):

i) A copy of the resolution of launching an offer taken by the offeror's competent bodies and of the necessary management decisions;

ii) Copies of both the offeror and of the issuer's by-laws;

iii) Updated certificates of commercial registration of both the offeror and the issuer;

iv) Copies of the management's annual and financial reports, reports from the auditing body as well as audit reports covering the issuer´s accounts for the last three tax years;

v) Copies of the management's annual and financial reports, reports from the auditing body as well as audit reports covering the offeror´s accounts for the last tax year;

vi) An auditor's report or statement on the offering;

vii) Copy of the contract entered into with the financial broker and of the placement/placement consortium contract, if applicable, as well as of the market placement/market stabilisation/greenshoe contracts, where appropriate;

viii) Draft public offer announcement and draft prospectus;

ix) Feasibility study, where required.

2.3.1.3. Feasibility Study

An economic and financial feasibility study of the issuer is also required where:

(i) The offer aims at the incorporation of a company by means of a public subscription;

(ii) The issuer has been operating for less than two years or has had losses in at least two of the last three financial years;

(iii) The calculation of the offer price is based mostly on the forecasts of the issuer´s future profitability.

2.3.1.4. Price Stabilisation

In case of launch of a public distribution offering, the offeror can establish that the price or, in the case of bonds, the interest rates, are determined by the last day prior to the assessment of the offering result, provided that the public offer announcement specifies the maximum and minimum limits of price variation and the objective criteria for its calculation.

The definitive prices or interest rates must be disclosed under the same conditions as the public distribution offering announcement and communicated to CMVM on the same day.

A price-stabilisation contract is allowed within a public distribution offering of securities, but can only be executed after the publishing of the announcement of the public distribution offering and up to thirty days after the assessment of its result.

2.3.1.5. Investment Intention's Invitation

Investment intention's invitation is permitted to determine the viability of an eventual public offer for distribution and can only be initiated after the disclosure of the preliminary prospectus. Investment invitation cannot serve as a means of entering into contracts, but may grant to those individuals consulted more favourable conditions in a future offer.

2.3.1.6. Partial Public Offer of Acquisition

The requirement to carry out a partial (i.e., over part of the target company's securities) mandatory takeover, set out in the now revoked Securities Code, was suppressed by the new Securities Code as it now requires all mandatory takeover bids to be launched for the totality of the target company's shares. The system of mandatory takeover bids, now in force, flows from the principle that minority shareholders must share the benefits brought about by the acquisition of control over a public company as well.

2.3.1.7. Thresholds of Mandatory Takeover Bids

Following the example of most similar legal systems, the thresholds for a mandatory takeover bid were set at one third or a half of the voting rights in the target company's share capital. As the system laid out in the now revoked Securities Market Code proved confusing with regard to the relevance of the acquisition of securities that confer the right to subscription or purchase of shares, the new Securities Code provides that only effective voting rights shall be taken into consideration when calculating the potential position of control of the offeror.

Mandatory (as well as compulsory) takeover bids for public companies have already been addressed in detail in the chapter "Corporate Governance" of this guide.

2.3.2. Financial Brokers

2.3.2.1. Financial Consulting

The Securities Code now allows the provision of financial consulting services - which was restricted to financial brokers - by independent advisers as well. The latter require an authorisation granted by CMVM. The Securities Code emphasises, in particular, the need for advisers to meet certain requirements of integrity and professional ability. Although independent advisers are not considered financial brokers, the former must comply with the regulations applicable to the latter's activities, adapted where appropriate.

2.3.2.2. Financial Intermediation Contracts

The regulation of financial intermediation contracts for the rendering of services is totally new in the Securities Code. These rules aim to protect investors, especially non-institutional investors, in the conclusion of agreements outside the scope of financial brokers. The system thereby laid out, applies only to the receipt of orders and the management of portfolios and is restricted to those cases where a previous client relationship does not exist and where the conclusion of the agreement has not been requested by the investor himself.

2.3.2.3. Specific Protection Granted to Non-institutional Investors with regard to Intermediation Contracts

As far as investor guarantees are concerned, the Securities Code differentiates between institutional and non- institutional investors, as the latter are granted specific protection. For the purposes of the Code, the following are considered institutional investors:

(i) Credit institutions;

(ii) Investment companies;

(iii) Collective investment institutions and their respective managing companies;

(iv) Insurance companies;

(v) Pension fund managing companies;

The Securities Code grants non-institutional investors the following guarantees:

i) Non-institutional investors may revoke brokerage contracts, which are subject to written form, if they fail to observe this requirement;

ii) Non-institutional investors benefit from the specific protection granted to consumers in regard of general contract clauses, since they are equated with consumers for such purpose;

iii) In brokerage contracts executed with non-institutional investors residing in Portugal, for the execution of operations in Portugal, application of the competent law cannot deprive the investor of the protection assured under the provisions of the Securities Code, regarding information, conflict of interests and asset separation;

iv) Orders for the execution of operations and for contracts of portfolio management issued or concluded by a non-institutional investor outside the financial broker's establishment, without a previous client relationship and without investor invitation, only come into effect three working days after the investor declares the transaction and, within this period, the investor may communicate a change of intention to the broker.

Public entities, public companies, holding companies, shareholders with a qualifying holding in a public company, independent advisers and collective entities do not benefit from the protection granted to non-institutional investors.

2.3.2.4. Specific Provisions on Negotiations by Financial Brokers on their own Account

Financial brokerage activities, undertaken by brokers on their own account, are considered investment services and are specifically regulated in the Securities Code. Regulated agreements are not the only agreements that a financial broker may conclude on his own account, as he is also allowed to enter into market making agreements, including price stabilisation agreements and securities lending.

2.3.3. Trading in Portugal of Securities issued by Foreign Entities

The new Securities Code sets out rules designed to allow and stimulate the trading in Portugal of securities issued by foreign entities.

2.3.3.1. Public Offers in the Portuguese Stock Market launched by Foreign Entities

Such offers are also subject to prior registration with the CMVM and, where they relate to securities issued by an entity subject to foreign law, a legal opinion certifying that the issuer is in good standing and that the securities were or will be issued in conformity with the applicable law, to be included in the prospectus, may be requested.

2.3.2.2. Prospectus of an International Offer

The Securities Code specifically provided for the prospectus of an international offer. Thus, where a public offer is made in various European Union (EU) Member States, the authority of the Member State where the issuer has its headquarters is empowered to approve the prospectus. Wherever the issuer is subject to foreign law, the prospectus must include a comparative note on the differences between the relevant foreign and Portuguese laws.

The Securities Code also enshrines the principle of mutual acceptance. Thus, the prospectus approved by the competent authority of an EU Member State related to a public offer launched simultaneously, or almost, in Portugal and in other Member States is valid for the effects of registration with the CMVM, as long as:

(i) It relates to securities issued by entities with their headquarters in EU Member States;

(ii) It includes information related to the institutions that provide the issuer's financial services, the tax regime, which the earnings from the offered securities are subject to in Portugal, and the form in which the notification to investors must be published.

(iii) It is translated into Portuguese.

2.3.3.3.   Listing of Foreign Securities on the Stock Exchange

The Securities Code sets out specific provisions on the admission to quotation in the Portuguese Stock Exchange of securities subject to a foreign law. Thus, unless the securities are admitted to trade in a regulated market located or operating in an EU Member State, the issuer must provide a legal opinion ensuring that the securities meet the requirements on content and form of representation set out in the applicable law and that the issuer was duly incorporated and it is in good standing in accordance with the prevailing law of their country of origin.

When the law of the State of the securities to be admitted to quotation does not allow their direct admission in a market located or operating outside this State, or the admission of these securities appears to be difficult for operational execution, representative certificates of registration or of deposit of these securities can be admitted to trade in a Stock Exchange located or operating in Portugal.

2.3.4. Securities held as Collateral

The new Securities Code implemented article 9(2) of European Parliament and Council Directive 98/26/EC of 19th May 1998, which adopts the international principle of the Place of Relevant Intermediary Approach (PRIMA) as the criterion for determining the law territorially applicable to the securities held as collateral. Decree-Law 221/2000 of 9th September 2000 later transposed Directive 98/26/EC's provisions with regard to the regulation of financial settlement systems.

The PRIMA principle means that when rights over securities are given as collateral to participants in a settlement system, central banks of the EU Member States or to the Central European Bank and are recorded in a register, account or centralised deposit system located in an EU Member State, the determination of the rights of such entities as holders of collateral in relation to those securities, shall be governed by the law of that Member State.

In accordance with the PRIMA principle, the Securities Code stipulates that, should securities given as collateral be registered or deposited in a centralised system, which is located or operating in a Member State of the EU, the determination of the rights of the guarantee's beneficiaries will be governed by the legislation of the same Member State.

On the other hand, and also in accordance with the PRIMA principle, the Code states that the transmission of rights and the establishment of collateral on securities that are registered or deposited, but not integrated into a E.U. centralised system, are governed by the laws of the State where those securities are registered or deposited.

The application of PRIMA aims at guaranteeing legal protection and certainty in the payments system and clearance operations of national and international securities. In addition, in implementing the PRIMA principle, the Securities Code envisaged the reduction in systemic risk by protecting the irreversibility of clearance and enforceability of guarantees provided by participants in the settlement system.

2.4. The Portuguese Stock Market

2.4.1. Market Structure

Pursuant to the Securities Code, the Stock Market can be structured into (a) Stock Exchanges; (b) other regulated markets and (c) non-regulated markets organised according to rules established by the respective managing entity.

The Portuguese Stock Market is currently structured as follows:
(i) Regulated markets: the stock exchange.
(ii) Non-regulated markets: the unlisted market (*Mercado sem Cotações*).
(iii) Trade outside a regulated market (off-the counter operations): repos and securities lending.

2.4.2. The Stock Exchange

The Portuguese stock exchange is managed by Euronext Lisbon, which resulted from the merger - closed in, and effective as of, 5th February 2002 - between Euronext NV (which is comprised of the Amsterdam, Brussels and Paris Exchanges and also of LIFFE - London International Financial Futures Exchange) and "BVLP - *Entidade Gestora de Mercados Regulamentados, S.A.*", which managed the former Lisbon and Oporto stock exchanges. Euronext Portugal is comprised of the following markets:

(i) Cash market;

(ii) Derivatives market;

(iii) Other markets (the MEOP - *Mercado Especial de Operações por Grosso* (Retail Operations Special Market) and the *MEDIP - Mercado Especial de Dívida Pública* (Public Debt Special Market));

2.4.2.1. Cash Market

The Euronext Portugal cash market is concentrated in the former Lisbon Stock Exchange and consists of the following segments:

(i) The main market;

(ii) The second market;

(iii) The unlisted market;

(iv) The new market.

The main market is the official quotation market, where shares, bonds, and other securities are traded alongside investment fund units, autonomous warrants and public sector debt securities; admission thereto is subject to tight requirements as regards financial and economic performance and share liquidity and to prior permission by Euronext Portugal as well as to the publication of a prospectus approved by the Stock Market Supervisory Authority (*Comissão do Mercado de Valores Mobiliários* - CMVM).

The second market is a forum for trading securities issued by companies. which do not meet the requirements for, or were excluded from, quotation on the main market (small and medium companies); requirements for admission thereto are lighter than those for admission to the main market.

The unlisted market is an unregulated market created for trading securities issued by companies that do not meet the requirements for, or were excluded from, quotation in either the main market or the second market.

The new market was created for trading securities issued by companies operating in the so-called "new economy" field.

2.4.2.2. Derivatives Market

Derivatives are traded in the former *Bolsa de Derivados do Porto* (Oporto Derivatives Market), created in 1996. Its managing body, the *Associação da Bolsa de Valores do Porto* (Oporto Stock Exchange Association) merged in 1999 with the *Associação da Bolsa de Valores de Lisboa* (Oporto Stock Exchange Association) to create BVLP, now Euronext Lisbon.

2.4.2.2.1. Legal Framework

The main legal regulations applicable to the derivatives market are the following:

i)   The Securities Code, whose provisions on securities also apply to derivative financial instruments, where appropriate;

ii) Ministry of Finance orders relating to Futures and Options contracts on commodities, services and currency and to any other types of forward transactions not regulated in the Securities Code;

iii) Stock Market Supervisory Authority (CMVM) regulations, including those on the futures and options market (market structure and membership), as well as on contracts, trading, clearing and fees;

(iv) Euronext Lisbon Internal Technical Regulations on membership requirements, the trading system, the safety system and on failure consequences.

(v) Euronext Lisbon's communications concerning technical details on futures and options trading.

2.4.2.2.2. Clearing, Settlement and Prudential Rules

Euronext Lisbon includes a Clearing House (Interbolsa, S.A.), which acts as the sole counterpart for every buyer and seller and is responsible for the successful conclusion of all transactions as well as for the registration, settlement, clearing, closing or transferring of any positions and the granting of necessary safety guarantees.

The safety system for futures and options transactions comprises of the following levels:

i) Daily calculation of settlement prices at the closing of each trading session;

ii) Application on futures and options settlements of initial, spread and extraordinary margins as well of indicative levels for price fluctuations in order to cover potential losses;

iii) Daily Operational Limit on trading allowed to each clearing member (i.e., trader admitted to settlement operations), calculated with regard to the amount of the Permanent Guarantee deposited by that clearing member;

iv) Additional Clearing Guarantee (ACG) - a mutual fund based on additional deposits by clearing members.

2.4.2.2.3. Types of Derivatives traded in Euronext

The following four types of derivative financial instruments are traded in Euronext Lisbon:

(i) **PSI-20 Futures contract** - a futures contract based on the PSI-20 Stock Exchange index. The PSI-20 is the benchmark for Euronext Lisbon and is comprised of the twenty most liquid and representative shares traded in the main market.

(ii) **Stock Futures contract** – a futures contracts based on the purchase and sale of 100-share in companies quoted on the main market. Euronext Lisbon is now trading *Portugal Telecom* (PT), *Electricidade de Portugal* - EDP, *Banco Comercial Português* - BCP, Cimpor, PT Multimedia, Sonae and Telecel Stock Futures.

(iii) **Stock Options contracts** – the purchase and sale of options on shareholdings in the main market quoted companies. Euronext currently trades Stock Options on Portugal Telecom, EDP, PT Multimedia, Sonae and Telecel.

2.4.2.3. Other Regulated Markets

Euronext is also comprised of two other regulated markets: the MEOP - *Mercado Especial de Operações por Grosso* (Retail Operations Special Market), a cash market created for the trading of large (worth a minimum 50 million euro each) blocks of shares in companies quoted on the main market, and the *MEDIP - Mercado Especial de Dívida Pública* (Public Debt Special Market), for trade in book-entry public sector bonds alone.

2.4.3. "Off-the-Counter" Operations

Euronext also provides registration, clearing and settlement services with regard to the following "off-the counter" (i.e., outside a regulated market) service:

a) **REPO (Repurchase Agreement)** - a REPO is an agreement whereby a party sells securities to another and simultaneously undertakes to unconditionally repurchase (while the purchaser undertakes to resell) those securities on a specified future date at a specified price. The purchaser then returns the securities to the seller and recovers the purchase price plus an interest rate. Thus, a REPO is a financing operation in which the underlying securities serve as collateral.

b) **Securities lending Transactions** – these types of transactions consist of an agreement whereby the lender makes certain securities available to the borrower, for a specified period of time. In return, the borrower gives the lender a collateral (guarantee) and pays him a fee.

2.4.4. Regulators and Supervisors

The Portuguese Stock Market is supervised and/or regulated by the following entities:

a) **Ministry of Finance** – it provides the main guidelines on Stock Market operations as well as on transactions not covered by the Securities Code;

b) **Stock Market Supervisory Authority** (*Comissão do Mercado de Valores Mobiliários*) – it is empowered to issue regulations on the requirements for admission and trade in the Stock Market as well as to approve most operations carried out therein;

c) **Bank of Portugal** (*Banco de Portugal*) - the Bank of Portugal is empowered to supervise money market and currency instruments as well to advise the Ministry of Finance on the guidelines on Stock Market operations as well as to approve, in conjunction with CMVM, the futures and options contracts that are traded by Euronext Lisbon.

COMMERCIAL CONTRACTS
CHAPTER 3

3.1. Introduction

Commercial contracts are the foundation for the way all business is conducted.

Regardless of the nature of the business, there will inevitably be areas where commercial contracts are relevant and desirable to assist in the smooth running of the operation. Commercial contracts are used to formalise relationships and to promote certainty in business transactions between suppliers, manufacturers, agents, distributors and, ultimately, customers. It is of utmost importance to have up-to-date commercial agreements governing your business relationships.

Among the plethora of commercial contracts currently available and used in Portugal the specific frameworks of the following categories are analysed:(i) consortium, (ii) unincorporated partnership, (iii) agency agreement, (iv) franchising agreement, (v) intermediation agreement, (vi) commercial concession agreement, (vii) leasing.

3.2. Consortium (*"Contrato de Consórcio"*)

A type of contract commonly utilised in Portugal for joint ventures is the so-called "consortium", under which two or more parties undertake to carry out jointly a certain activity or to act in concert in order to achieve a common purpose.

3.2.1. Legal Framework

Consortia are regulated by Decree-Law 231/81, of 28th July 1981.

3.2.2. Main Characteristics

Consortia can be formed for the purpose of preparing and/or implementing a given project or undertaking, supplying goods to third parties, promoting research, exploiting natural resources, or producing goods to be shared amongst the members of the consortium.

The objective of the consortium must be well defined in the respective agreement and the obligations of the parties must be clearly set forth therein, as well as any contributions and share of common expenses.

Consortium members are obliged to (a) abstain from competing with the consortium itself, (b) provide the other consortium members with all relevant information and (c) allow the examination of the goods supplied or the activities carried out within the consortium.

Consortium members are also required to nominate a "head of consortium" (who leads the consortium) among them and may optionally instate a "supervisory board" comprised of all consortium members.

3.2.3. Form of Agreement

The formation of a consortium requires a written agreement. If, amongst the members of the consortium, there is a transfer of property for the venture, then the consortium will only be valid if executed by means of a notarial deed.

3.2.4. Termination of the Consortium

The consortium is terminated where:

(i) Unanimously agreed to by its members;

(ii) Its object is accomplished;

(iii) The time limit set out for the agreement's validity is achieved, unless extended by the members;

(iv) All but a single member remains in the consortium;

(v) Any other cause set forth in the consortium agreement is verified;

(vi) Should none of the above apply, within ten years of the date the consortium agreement was signed, without prejudice to time limit extensions agreed by the consortium members.

3.3. Unincorporated Partnership ("*Contrato de Associação em Participação*")

Another type of contract utilised in Portugal as an alternative to the classic incorporation of companies or consortia is an unincorporated partnership agreement ("*contrato de associação em participação*" or "*contrato de conta em participação*"), pursuant to which one or more persons or entities (hidden partners) share the profits or profits and losses incurred by another person or entity (operational partner) in carrying out a certain commercial activity.

3.3.1. Legal Framework

The unincorporated partnership agreement is also regulated by Decree-law 231/81, of 28th July 1981, referred to above.

3.3.2. Main Characteristics of the Unincorporated Partnership Agreement

The hidden partner shares the profits or profits and losses (sharing the losses is optional) incurred by the operational partner in the activity covered by the agreement, in return for a contribution, which may consist of capital, goods or rights. Such a contribution can be replaced by reciprocal unincorporated partnership agreements, concluded simultaneously.

The agreement must specify the "hidden partner"'s share in the operational   partner's profits or profits and losses with regard to the activity covered by the agreement. However, the hidden partner's share in such losses cannot be higher than their proportionate contribution.

3.3.3. Form of Agreement

This type of agreement is not subject to any specific format, unless otherwise required by law with regard to the nature of the assets contributed by the hidden partner to the partnership.

3.3.4.Termination of the Partnership

The unincorporated partnership is terminated wherever any cause as set forth in the respective agreement is verified as well as on the following grounds: i) if the partnership's object is fully accomplished or such accomplishment becomes impossible; ii) upon the death of any of the partners, if expressly wished by his successors; iii) if one of the partners, being a company, is liquidated; iv) if one of the partners attains the position of both operational and hidden partner; v) termination by any of the partners on grounds of just cause; and vi) if any of the partners goes bankrupt or insolvent.

3.4. Agency Agreement ("*Contrato de Agência*")

3.4.1. Legal Framework

The agency agreement, or commercial representation agreement, as it is also called, is regulated by Decree-Law 178/86, of 3 July 1986, as amended by Decree-Law 118/93 of 13 April 1993, which implemented Council Directive 86/653/EEC of 18 December 1986.

3.4.2. Main Characteristics

According to the definition set out in the abovementioned regulations, an agency agreement is one whereby a person (the agent) undertakes to negotiate on behalf of another person (the principal) certain contracts within a certain territory or amongst a specific group of clients, in an autonomous and stable manner, and for a certain consideration (usually a commission).

3.4.3. Form of Agreement

A specific form for agency agreements in Portugal is not required. However, the following clauses are valid only if they are laid down in writing:

i)   Those whereby the agent is empowered to conclude contracts on behalf and in the name of the principal;

ii)   Those whereby the agent is empowered to collect debts on behalf and in the name of the principal (such empowerment is presumed if the agent is already empowered to conclude contracts on behalf and in the name of the principal);

iii)   Those establishing the agency's exclusivity;

iv)   "*Del credere*" arrangements;

v)   Restraint of trade clause;

vi)   Termination of the agreement by mutual consent;

vii)   Termination of the agreement by one of the parties.

3.4.4. "*Del credere*" Arrangement

Under the "*del credere*" arrangement, the agent undertakes to guarantee the execution of a certain contract concluded between the principal and a third person, provided that the contract was negotiated or concluded by the agent. Such an arrangement is only valid if laid down in writing and if it either specifies the contract whose execution is thereby guaranteed or indicates the person to whom the guarantee relates.

3.4.5. Restraint of Trade Clause

Under a restraint of trade clause the agent undertakes to refrain from business activities which may compete with those pursued by the principal for a certain period of time after termination of the agency agreement. Such a clause must be laid down in writing and is valid for a maximum two-year period and only for activities involving the agent's group of clients or territory.

3.4.6. Professional Secrecy

The agent cannot divulge or make personal use of the secrets which the principal has confided to him or of which he has become aware as a result of exercising his activity, even after termination of the contract.

3.4.7. The Use of Sub-agents

Recourse to sub-agents is allowed unless otherwise agreed by the parties. The sub-agency agreement is also regulated by Decree-Law 178/86 of 3rd July 1986, with the appropriate adaptations.

3.4.8. Right to Information

The principal is obliged to inform the agent, without delay, whether he accepts the contracts negotiated as well as those concluded by the agent without being empowered to do so.

The principal should supply the agent with periodical listings of the contracts concluded and commissions due as well as all the information the agent needs to verify the commissions he is entitled to.

3.4.9. Exclusivity

Wherever it is established that the agency is to be exclusive, the principal may not use other agents to carry out activities competing with those of the agent within the area or group of clients allocated to that agent.

3.4.10. Termination of the Agency Agreement

The agency agreement terminates upon expiry of the fixed period agreed by the parties, via the verification of a resolving condition if such a condition was agreed by the parties, or upon the death of the agent.

Only agency agreements concluded for an undetermined period of time can be terminated by either party, by serving a termination notice in writing to the other party.

3.4.10.1. Period of Notice

The period of notice is of one month, two months and three months for the first year, second year and third and subsequent years of the agreement, respectively.
Failure by either party to comply with the period of notice entitles the other party to compensation.

3.4.10.2. Rescission of the agreement

The agency agreement can be rescinded immediately by either party in case of breach of contract by the other party if, as a result thereof, the operation of the agreement is no longer possible or where such circumstances occur that gravely hinder or render impossible the operation of the agreement until the end of the fixed period or the date of termination resulting from the applicable period of notice.

3.4.11. Claim to Compensation for Breach of Contract

Irrespective of the right to terminate the agreement, either party is entitled to compensation for damages arising from the other party's breach of the obligations arising from the agreement.

3.4.12. Claim to Compensation for Termination

Irrespective of his right to compensation mentioned above, upon termination of the contract the agent is entitled to "clientele compensation", provided that:

(i) He was responsible for attracting new clients or has significantly increased the volume of business with existing clients;

(ii) The principal derives a significant benefit from the agent's activity after termination of the contract; and

(iii) The agent has lost commissions on negotiated contracts as a result of the termination of the agreement.

3.5. Franchising Agreement ("*Contrato de Franquia*")

3.5.1. Legal Framework

3.5.1.1. Portuguese Legislation

Although franchising agreements are widely utilised in Portugal, there is no national legislation dealing with them specifically. Of particular interest for this matter is the application of national legislation on competition (in this regard, please see comments on restrictive covenants in the chapter relating to competition and antitrust law).

3.5.1.2. European Union Legislation

Franchising agreements, particularly cross-border ones, must also comply with European Union competition law, namely article 81 of the EC Treaty on concerted practices and agreements between companies and community legislation implementing such provisions. Indeed, typical franchise agreement clauses, like those granting the franchisee exclusivity in a certain territory or exclusive access to the franchisor's know-how, may be deemed incompatible with article 81 of the EC Treaty.

The European Commission, however, recognised the importance of franchising as a means of economic development by optimising sales and investment and reducing costs. Thus, under its power to exempt by regulation certain categories of agreements from application of article 81 of the Treaty, the Commission adopted Regulation (EEC) No 4087/88 of 30th November 1988 on the application of article 85 (3) of the Treaty to categories of franchise agreements, which was later replaced by Commission Regulation (EC) no. 2790/1999 of 22nd December 1999 on the application of article 81(3) of the Treaty to categories of vertical agreements and concerted practices (*block exemptions*).

Furthermore, the European Franchising Federation (EFF) - a non-profit organisation comprised of the national franchise associations of several European countries - adopted the "European Code of Ethics for Franchising" ("*Código Europeu de Deontologia do Franchising*"), which sets out detailed criteria for franchising agreements, as well as detailed conditions to be observed by the contracting parties. EFF members undertake to impose on their own members the obligation to apply, and abide by, the provisions of the "European Code".

3.5.2. Main Characteristics

A franchising agreement is an agreement whereby a person (franchisor) authorises another person (franchisee) to utilise a trademark, logo or symbol belonging to the franchisor and to use his know-how, products or services. The franchisor provides technical assistance to the franchisee in connection with the licensed goods, against the payment of remuneration or fees by the franchisee. The agreement may be valid only for a certain territory.

3.5.3. Termination

The franchise agreement can be terminated pursuant to the general rules applicable to contracts in Portugal. Recourse to legal provisions on termination of agency agreements (referred to above) is admissible. However, that depends chiefly on the specific terms of the franchise agreement.

3.6. Intermediation Agreement ("*Contrato de Mediação*")

3.6.1. Legal Framework

Intermediation agreements in general are not regulated in Portugal; there are, however, certain types of intermediation agreement that have their own specific regulation, such as intermediation in the purchase and sale of property, which is regulated by Decree-Law 77/99, of 16th March 1999, as amended by Decree-Law 258/2001, or financial brokerage, which is regulated by Decree-Law 262/2001 of 28th September 2001 and Securities Market Supervisory Authority Regulation no. 12/2000 of 23rd February 2000.

3.6.2. Main Characteristics

A mediation agreement can be defined as an agreement pursuant to which one of the parties undertakes to find an interested party for a given business and to introduce this third party to the other party of the agreement, so that they can discuss the possibility of doing business. Contrary to the commissioner and the commercial agent, the mediator is not bound to any of the parties of the deal to which he provides his services.

3.6.3. Representation

In this regard, it is important to note that mediation does not involve representation of any of the parties, nor is the mediator dependent on any of the parties, as he actually acts in the interest of both parties and not for one of them alone.

3.6.4. Remuneration

The mediator only acquires the right to receive remuneration if the business is concluded following his intervention. Such remuneration often consists of a commission calculated on the basis of the value of the said business.

3.7. Commercial Concession ("*Contrato de Concessão Comercial*")

3.7.1. Legal Framework

This is another type of commercial agreement, which, although not identified in law, is widely used in Portugal. Commercial concession agreements are very similar to agency agreements and the Portuguese courts' case-law has consistently held that the legal framework for agency agreements, as defined by Decree-Law 178/86, of 3rd July 1986 as amended by Decree-Law 118/93 of 13th April 1993, also applies, by analogy, to commercial concession agreements.

This legal framework is very similar to the ones implemented in all other EU member States, because it is based on the Council Directive 86/653/CE of 18th December 1986.

3.7.2. Main Characteristics

The commercial concession agreement is the contract through which one of the parties (the grantee) undertakes to buy from the other party (the grantor) goods manufactured and/or distributed by the grantor so as to re-sell them within a specified zone. Usually, the grantee must pay a part of the profits obtained in such re-sales to the grantor. Under most concession agreements the grantee undertakes to re-sell the grantor's products exclusively.

3.7.3. Representation

Notwithstanding the above, commercial concession agreements differ from agency agreements as the grantee will always act on his own behalf and in his own name, acquiring the ownership of the goods so as to resell them to third parties and bearing all the risks of their commercialisation, whilst in the agency agreement the agent will always act on behalf of someone else.

3.7.4. Termination of the Contract

The termination of the contract without just cause entitles the damaged party to receive compensation for damages. Given the similarity between commercial concession agreements and agency agreements, termination of commercial concession agreements is often regulated with recourse to the application of the provisions on contract termination of the agency agreement's legal framework.

3.7.5. Compensation

Also in view of the abovementioned similarity between commercial concession agreements and agency agreements, Portuguese courts have already ruled on the obligation of the grantor to pay to the grantee compensation in view of results achieved by the grantee in the formation of clientele ("clientele compensation"), calculated in equitable terms, taking into consideration the benefits received by the grantor in view of the grantee's performance.

3.8. Leasing (*"Locação Financeira"*)

3.8.1. Legal Framework

This is a commercial contract which is often used for financing the purchase of real or movable property. It is regulated in Portugal by Decree-Law 149/95, of 24 June 1995 as amended by Decree-Law 265/97, of 2 October 1997 and by Decree-Law 285/2001 of 3rd November 2001.

3.8.2. Main Characteristics

A leasing agreement is an agreement whereby a person (lessor) supplies to another (lessee) property or equipment, acquired or built by the former under instructions given by the latter, against receipt of instalments paid by the same, whilst keeping the ownership of the goods until the end of the agreement.

The lessee has the option to acquire the equipment or property at the end of the agreement, by paying a so-called residual value, determined in accordance with the criteria laid out in the agreement, to the lessor. If the lessee chooses not to purchase the property or equipment, then the same will have to be returned, or the contract may be renewed.

3.8.3. Form of Agreement

Leasing agreements are usually private agreements. However, when a property is leased, the signatures of the parties as well as the existence of valid permission for the construction or the use of the property in question must be certified by a Notary Public; where a movable asset subject to mandatory registration (e.g., a car or a boat) is the object of the leasing agreement, complete details of each of the signatory's identity cards or the equivalent is required. In either case the agreement must be registered with the pertinent registration office.

3.8.4. Duration of the Agreement

Leasing agreements must have a term at most equal to the leased asset's estimated economic lifetime, up to a maximum of 30 years. In the absence of an indication of the agreement's term, the latter shall be presumed to be equal to 18 months (for movable assets) or 7 years (for immovable assets).

3.8.5. Termination of the Agreement

Agreements can be terminated by either party on grounds of breach of contract by the other party pursuant to the general rules on contracts contained in the Portuguese Civil Code.

However, the rules contain therein relating to rental agreements (which might easily apply to leasing agreements since both have common traits but impose heavy requirements for termination by the renter) do not apply to leasing agreements, as expressly determined by Decree-Law 149/95.

The agreement can also be terminated by the lessor upon the lessee's death or liquidation (if it is a legal entity) or upon verification of the lessee's bankruptcy. Anticipated termination of the agreement is also admissible where the lessee pays - with the lessor's approval - all the remaining instalments and the residual value.

COMPANY LAW

CHAPTER 4

4.1 Introduction

Company Law is a varied and fast moving field. New legislation is frequent, spurred by the twin pressures of the EU policy on harmonization of the laws of Member States, and by Member States Industry's own reformist zeal for making company law consistent with the realities of commercial life and reflective of current Government social and economic policies.

Company Law is the backbone of modern business, it covers virtually every aspect of running a company, including the legal norms concerning the establishing, organising, operating and managing of limited liability companies and joint stock companies. The quality of company law is also of central importance to the development of efficient capital markets.

4.2 Applicable Law

Portuguese companies are regulated by the Portuguese Companies Code, enacted by Decree-Law 262/86 of 2nd September 1986, as amended, and by additional laws and regulations.

4.2.1. Conflicts of Jurisdiction

According to the Portuguese Companies Code, and International Private Companies Law General Principles, the law applicable to corporate entities is the law of the place where they have their head office and their main place of business. However, if those companies have their statutory head office in Portugal they are subject to Portuguese jurisdiction, even if their main place of business is situated abroad.

Companies that have their head-office abroad but wish to conduct business in Portugal for more than one year, must establish a permanent representation in Portugal, which will be governed by Portuguese law.

4.3. Steps to Incorporate a Company in Portugal

The incorporation of companies in Portugal requires the following steps:

i) Corporate name certificate:

- A corporate name certificate must be applied for at the Company Names Registrar (*Registo Nacional de Pessoas Colectivas*), and must reflect the company's indented activities, as well as not be misleading as regards the identification of the shareholders or be prone to being confused with another name already registered.

- The principle of exclusivity will protect the corporate name in the Portugal.

- A certificate of registration, as well as a provisional tax registration card will be issued by the Company Names Registrar.

ii) Deposit of share capital:

- The share capital, or the part thereof legally required to be paid immediately. must be deposited with a Portuguese Bank

iii) Articles of Association and deed of incorporation:

- The Articles of Association must be drawn up, and the deed of incorporation must be executed and then signed and sealed by a notary public.

- The deed may be contained in a private document only, if the company to be incorporated is a 'sole quotaholder company'[1] (*sociedade unipessoal por quotas*) whose share capital is entirely paid-up in cash or in assets for whose transfer a notarial deed is not required.

iv) Registration with the Tax Authorities:

- The shareholders must apply for the registration of the commencement of activities with the local Tax Authorities, and this application must be signed by the auditor that will henceforth be responsible for the accounts of the company

v) Registration with the Commercial Companies' Registrar:

- The deed of incorporation must be registered at the Commercial Companies' Registrar and this entity will also proceed with the publication of the deed of constitution in the Portuguese official gazette, and only then shall the company be fully incorporated

vi) Social Security:

- The company must also be registered for social security purposes

4.4. Most Common Types of Companies – Private Companies

The types of companies most frequently adopted in Portugal are:

1. Private limited quota companies (*Limitadas*)

2. Sole quotaholder companies (*Unipessoais de quotas*)

3. Joint Stock Companies (*Sociedades anónimas*)

4.4.1 Private Limited Quota Companies (Limitada)

---

[1] *A sole quotaholder company (sociedade unipessoal por quotas) is a private limited liability company controlled by a single quotaholder who owns the totality of the company's share capital, which is divided into 'quotas'.*

71

This type of company is the most common, simple and financially sound answer for small and medium sized enterprises. Its share capital is divided proportionally into quotas (a type of shareholding which is subject to registration with the Companies' Registry and the transfer subject to public deed). The quotas must be registered, but are not represented by securities or certificates. As laid out below, quotas transfer can be restricted by the company's Articles of Association, and/or by shareholder agreement. Shareholders ("quotaholders") are jointly and severally liable for the paying up the share capital, but they are only liable up to the amount of that share capital. The word " Limitada" (limited), which must be present in the trade name, refers to the fact that only the company's assets can be used to pay the creditors in case of debt or bankruptcy.

To incorporate a limited quota company, there must be, at least, two quotaholders, with the exception of the sole quotaholder companies, and a share capital of 5000 Euros divided into blocks with a value of no less than 100 Euros each, that is, of no less than 2% of the share capital.

The share capital can be paid up in cash alone or in cash and assets, which must be specified and evaluated by a *revisor oficial de contas* – a qualified auditor. Cash payments can be partially postponed, up to a maximum 55% thereof.

Where the capital is paid partly in assets, the total sum of the cash payment made immediately and the value of the assets cannot be lower than the statutory minimum share capital.

In accordance with the Portuguese Companies Code, the transfer of a holding must be effected by means of a public deed, except when such a transfer occurs as part of a judicial procedure.

A quota cannot be transferred without prior consent of the company, except where the transfer is in favour of a spouse, parents, children or amongst quotaholders.

The company's consent must be requested by the transferor prior to the transfer and given in a general meeting resolution. Under certain circumstances, the refusal of such consent is of a pre-emptive character, that is to say the transfer is ineffective. Such refusal must be accompanied by an acquisition offer to the transferor.

Quotaholders may introduce into the Articles of Association certain limitations regarding free transmission of quotas or specific requirements to obtain the company's consent, or even forbidding the transfer of quotas.

4.4.1.1. Corporate Bodies:

i) Directors – The management of the company is assigned to one or more directors who may or may not be quotaholders. The directors may be nominated in the Articles of Association or by a resolution of the quotaholders. The Articles of Association may, however, require different or additional steps to nominate the directors of the company. Quotaholders will always be entitled to remove directors except if they are themselves shareholders and have a special right to their position. In such a case, removal must occur with the express consent of the Director in question or by just cause.

The directors of a company must be individuals. If a legal entity is elected as a director, it must nominate an individual who will represent it in his or her own name.

ii) General Meeting – The general meeting makes all relevant decisions in the life of the company whilst the directors make day-to-day decisions necessary to manage the business and perform all tasks that are not assigned to any other body of the company.

iii) Auditing – Auditing is optional in a limited quota company. However, those companies which do not have a board of auditors are required to appoint a qualified auditor (*Revisor Oficial de Contas*) if two of the following limits are surpassed, for two consecutive years:

    a)   Total net assets: 1,500,000 Euros;

    b)   Total of the net sails and other profits: 3,000,000 Euros;

    c)   Number of employees: 50.

4.4.1.2. Distribution of Profits

Quotaholders have the right to share in the profits in relation to the proportion of their contribution to the capital. At least half of the company's profits must be distributed to the quotaholders, notwithstanding the legal limitations thereto in regard of the legal reserve and of company solvency.

The Articles of Association or a resolution made by a majority of three quarters of the share capital at a general meeting convened for that purpose may stipulate exceptions to the abovementioned rule.

4.4.1.2.1. Distribution of Profits before the Year-end Results

It is possible to distribute profits before the year-end results. For this distribution, the private limited quota companies, must comply with the legal and accountancy requirements set out in section 4.4.3.4.1., below, for joint stock companies.

4.4.1.3. Dissolution

The dissolution of a company will occur whenever:

i)   Stipulated in the Articles of Association;

ii)   Agreed in a resolution passed at a general meeting by a majority of three quarters of the voting rights corresponding to the capital, which cannot be overridden by the Articles of Association;

iii)   The company's objective was entirely fulfilled or subsequently declared illegal;

iv)   The company was declared bankrupt;

v)   Determined by a court of law or by a general meeting resolution approved by a simple majority where:

-        the number of quotaholders remains below the minimum legally required for more than a year;

-        fulfilling the company's objective is deemed impossible;

-        the company has had no *de facto* activity for five consecutive years;

-        the company carries out an activity that is not included in its corporate objective.

4.4.1.4. Winding Up

The winding up of the company occurs by effect of the dissolution and entails the full settlement of the company's debts and the division of its remaining assets between the quotaholders.

4.4.2 Sole Quotaholder Company

These types of companies are a form of limited quota companies and may be incorporated from the beginning by a single quotaholder or, having been a limited quota company, are subsequently transformed into a single quotaholder company, by concentrating all of the capital in a single quotaholding, irrespective of the form and motive for such concentration.

For this transformation to take place, such an intention must be declared either in the deed through which the sole quotaholder acquires the remaining quotas of the company, or in a deed of transformation, which can be replaced by a private document where none of the company's assets require a notarial deed to be transferred.

According to the Portuguese Companies Code, decisions will be made by the sole quotaholder alone, and must be registered in the minutes book and signed by him/her.

Article 270 F gives the sole quotaholder the possibility, if expressly permitted by the Articles of Association, of entering into legal agreements with the company itself with the purpose of carrying out the company's objectives.

4.4.3 Joint Stock Companies

In order to incorporate a joint stock company, the Companies Code requires the existence of at least five shareholders and a minimum share capital of 50,000 Euros, divided into shares with a value of no less than one cent of a Euro each.

The share capital can be paid up in cash alone or in cash and assets. The latter must be specified and evaluated by a qualified auditor and its payment cannot be postponed. If it is paid up in cash alone, it can be postponed up to a maximum of 70% for a period of no more than five years, while the remaining 30% must be paid up immediately.

4.4.3.1.Types of Shares

Shares can be bearer shares or nominative shares. They must be nominative where:

a) They are not entirely paid up;

b) The Articles of Association impose restrictions on their transmission, including the need for prior authorisation of the company;

c) The shareholder is obliged, according to the Articles of Association, to render to the company any supplementary contributions.

Shares may also be classified in accordance with the rights attached thereto:

i) Common Shares – Holders are entitled to all the rights and duties prescribed by law;

ii) Non – Voting Preference Shares – These shares do not confer on their holders any voting rights but entitle them to a dividend of no less than 5% of their value, paid in preference to any other share, as long as they do not exceed 50% of the share capital;

77

iii)   Redeemable Preference Shares – Preference shares may benefit from a premium, and the company has the right to redeem these shares whenever the general meeting decides to do so, or on a set date.

4.4.3.2. Transfer of Shares

There is no specific contractual form for the purchase and sale of shares. However, a record must be kept of the shares issued by joint stock companies.

The transfer of shares cannot be forbidden and can only be restricted by the company's Articles of Association where permitted by law. Thus, these may impose, in regard of the transmission of nominative shares such restrictions as pre-emption rights conferred to other shareholders, the need for prior consent from the company or compliance with specific requirements deemed to be in the company's interest.

4.4.3.3. Bonds

Provided that the corporation's Articles of Association have been registered at least two years in advance and that the two last balance sheets were duly approved, the corporation may issue bonds, as long as those do not exceed the paid up share capital.

Some of the following types of bonds may be issued:

i)   Bonds that grant their holder the right to a fixed interest rate and provide a supplementary interest on a refundable premium, pre-agreed or depending on the company's profits;

ii)   Bonds that grant the holder the right to interest and provide for a redemption plan, both in accordance with the issuer's profits;

iii)   Bonds that provide a premium on issue;

iv)   Bonds that may be converted into shares or entitle their holders to acquire one or more shares.

4.4.3.4. Corporate Bodies

4.4.3.4.1. Management Structure

According to the Portuguese Companies Code, corporations must adopt either of two management structures:

a)   A unitary structure, which consists of a *Conselho de Administração* (board of directors) or, in certain cases, a single Director, overseen by a *Conselho Fiscal* (board of auditors); or

b)   A dual structure in which management powers are shared between a single manager or a board of a maximum 5 managers and a *Conselho Geral* (advisory board), overseen by a sole qualified auditor.

The dual structure has had little success in Portugal; most companies prefer the unitary structure.

4.4.3.4.1.1. Unitary Management Structure

4.4.3.4.1.1.1. Board of Directors/Single Director

a)   Composition and Nomination

The board of directors must be composed of an odd number of members. These are nominated either in the Articles of Association themselves or at a general meeting of shareholders.

Corporations whose share capital does not exceed 200,000 euros can nominate a single Director instead of a board of directors.

b)   Powers of the Board of Directors/Single Director

The board of directors or single director is empowered to:

(i) Manage and conduct, in general, the business of the corporation, subject to decisions taken by shareholders at general meetings, or to the intervention of the board of auditors, where required by the law or the Articles of Association;

(ii) Elect the Chairman of the board and co-opt board members;

(iii) Convene general meetings;

(iv) Produce the annual report;

(v) Decide on purchase, sale or encumbrance of fixed assets;

(vi) Grant guarantees on behalf of the company;

(vii) Decide on restructuring the company and/or its activities;

(viii) Relocation of the company's registered offices and increase of the company's share capital;

(ix) Make, or elaborate on, proposals for the merger, demerger or transformation of the corporation;

(x) Make decisions on any matters as established in the Articles of Association.

c) Delegation of Powers

The corporation's Articles of Association may authorise the board of directors to delegate day-to-day management decisions to a *Comissão Executiva* (executive committee) formed by an odd number of members of the board.

Upon creating the *Comissão Executiva*, the board of directors must define its composition, procedures and powers, which cannot include those referred to in items (i), (ii), (iii), (iv), (vi), (viii), (ix) of paragraph b) above.

4.4.3.4.1.1.2. Board of Auditors

Corporations are required to nominate either a board of auditors or a sole auditor.

The board of auditors must have either three full members and one alternate member or five full members and two alternate members. One of the members and one of the alternates must be either a qualified auditor *(Revisor Oficial de Contas)* or a qualified auditing firm (the so-called *Sociedade de Revisores Oficiais de Contas*) and cannot be shareholders.

If the corporation nominates a sole auditor, it is required to nominate an alternate auditor as well. Each one of them must be a qualified auditor or a qualified auditing firm.

The board of auditors /sole auditor is empowered, *inter alia*, (i) to oversee the managing body's activities as well as the company's books and accounts, (ii) to deliver an opinion on the management's annual report and, (iii) to certify the company's books and accounts for tax and administrative authorities.

4.4.3.4.1.2.Dual Management Structure

4.4.3.4.1.2.1. Managers

Corporations which adopt the dual management structure are required to nominate either a single manager (if they have a share capital under 200,000 euros) or a board of a maximum five managers. Managers are nominated in the Articles of Association or at a general meeting and must be individuals not members of the advisory board (Conselho *Geral*) or members of boards of auditors of companies which stand in a controlling or affiliated relationship with the company in question, or relatives of incumbent managers.

The single manager or board of managers has full management powers, including those described in item 4.4.3.4.1.1.1. b) above, as well as full powers to act on behalf of the corporation.

4.4.3.4.1.2.2. Advisory Board (*"Conselho Geral"*)

The members of the advisory board are nominated in the Articles of Association by the general meeting and must outnumber the managers, up to a maximum 15 members.
The advisory board is empowered to, *inter alia*:
(i)   Examine the company's books and accounts;
(ii) Oversee the managers' activities and approve the annual report submitted by those managers;
(iii) Submit an annual report on its own activities to the shareholders;
(iv) Grant or deny its consent to share transfers wherever such consent is required by the Articles of Association;
(v) Convene general meetings whenever appropriate.

4.4.3.4.1.2.3. Sole Auditor

The sole auditor is nominated by the general meeting and must be either a qualified auditor or a qualified auditing firm.
The sole auditor's powers and duties are the same as the board of auditors in the unitary management structure.

4.4.3.4.2. Company Secretary (*"Secretário da Sociedade"*)

Corporations quoted on the Stock Exchange are required to nominate a *Secretário da Sociedade* (Company Secretary) and a substitute. Such nomination is optional for non-quoted corporations and *limitada* companies.

The Secretary is nominated either upon the incorporation of the company or by the board or directors or managers and is empowered to, *inter alia*:

(i) Assist general meetings as well as those of the board of directors, advisory board and managers and record their respective minutes;

(ii) Keep the minutes book as well as the share registration book;

(iii) Certify copies of company records, including the minutes of general meetings and the Articles of Association, wherever such copies are requested by shareholders.

4.4.3.4.3. General Meetings

General meetings take place whenever they are convened by the board of directors or managers, by the board of auditors or by shareholders holding at least 5% of the share capital.

General meetings are empowered to:

(i) Approve the annual report where it is the competent corporate body to do so;

(ii) To decide on the board of directors' proposals, approved by the board of auditors, on profit reinvestment;

(iii) To oversee and nominate or remove the members of corporate bodies, including the board of directors and the board of auditors;

(iv) Decide on increases or decreases in the share capital, merging, demerging, or transforming the company as well as amendments to the Articles of Association;

(v) Decide on matters specified by the Articles of Association.

Each shareholder has one vote per share, except where otherwise set out in the Articles of Association, which can (a) award a vote per block of shares equivalent to a minimum 1,000 euros of the share capital (b) restrict the maximum number of votes cast per shareholder, either in his own name or on behalf of another shareholder (*voting cap*).

A *quorum* for a general meeting is only required where determined by the Articles of Association or where it is convened to decide on any of the subjects referred to in item (iv) above. In this case a *quorum* of a minimum one-third of the share capital is required.

Resolutions are approved by a simple majority, unless the Articles of Association require otherwise or they relate to any of the subjects referred to in item (iv), as in this case a two-thirds majority of the votes cast is required.

4.4.3.4. Distribution of Profits

Shareholders have the right to share in the profits of the company and so at least half of the yearly profits must be distributed to them, notwithstanding the legal limitations as regards the legal reserve and of company solvency.

The Articles of Association, as well as resolutions passed by three quarters of the votes at a general meeting, may stipulate different rules for the distribution of profits.

4.4.3.5.1. Distribution of Profits before the Year-end Results

It is possible to distribute profits before the year end results provided that this is permitted in the Articles of Association, such distribution is effected only in the second half of the year and that it conforms with the following legal and accountancy steps:

- Resolution of the management and the auditor's or board of auditors' consent, following the production of a mid term balance sheet produced in the previous thirty days which has been certified by the qualified auditor, attesting to the existence of distributable profits, notwithstanding the statutory limitations concerning legal reserves and company solvency.

Such a distribution of profits can be effected only once during the fiscal year.

4.4.3.6. Dissolution

The rules for dissolution of limited quota companies apply for the dissolution of joint stock companies, but if it is a resolution of a general meeting, which determines the dissolution, a minimum of one third of the share capital quorum is required, and a two thirds majority must approve the decision.

4.4.3.7. Winding Up

The winding up of the company occurs as a consequence of the dissolution and entails the full settlement of the corporation's debts and the division of its remaining assets between shareholders.

4.5. Specific Types of Companies

As stated above, specific types of companies in Portugal, such as Pure Holding Companies and Public Companies, are regulated outside the Portuguese Companies Code although its provisions are also applicable to them.

4.5.1. Pure Holding Companies (SGPS)

Pure Holding Companies ("*Sociedades Gestoras de Participações Sociais*") are companies whose corporate object consists solely of managing holdings in other companies, and are specially regulated by Decree-Law 495/88, of 30th December 1988, as amended, and the Portuguese Companies Code, where applicable.

However, pure holding companies, can, nevertheless, hold less than 10% of the share capital in a particular company they invest in, under the following circumstances:

a) Where the total amount of such holdings does not exceed 30% of the total amount of the holdings mentioned above; or

b) Where each one of them was acquired for no less than 5,000,000 € (Euros); or

c) Where the acquisition followed a merger or demerger of those companies; or

Where the acquisition was effected by a company which concluded an agreement with the holding company whereby it is managed in accordance with the instructions given by the latter.

As mentioned above, pure holding companies are prohibited from disposing of, or encumbering, their shareholdings held for less than a year, except where acquired by exchange or where the respective capital gains are reinvested within six months.

Pure holding companies are also prohibited from owning immovable assets, except for their own premises, as well as, granting loans to companies other than those they invest in.

Finally, pure holding companies, must be incorporated as either a private limited quota companies (sociedades por quotas) or joint stock companies (sociedades anónimas) and their corporate names must include the expression *Sociedade Gestora de Participações Sociais or SGPS.*

4.5.2. Public Companies

Public companies ("Sociedades Abertas") are companies open for public investment and listed on the Stock Exchange, or whose shares are the subject of a public offer for sale on the Stock Exchange.

These companies are regulated by the Companies Code and the Portuguese Securities Code (Decree-Law 486/99 of 13th November 1999, as amended).

4.6. Corporate Relationships: Affiliated Companies

The most common forms of corporate relationships are affiliated relationships, as follows:

4.6.1. Holdings

A company that holds at least 10% of the share capital of another and must inform the other of any transactions involving its holdings made since acquiring the qualifying holding

4.6.2. Mutual Holdings

Two companies that own holdings of at least 10% of each other's share capital, and that have a mutual duty of information.

4.6.3 Controlling Relationship

Where a company exercises a dominant influence over another company, dominance that may be presumed where the first company owns the majority of the other's share capital or voting rights, or where it can nominate more than half of the members of the board of director's from the other company

4.6.4. Group Relationship

A company that holds the totality of another company's share capital.

4.7. Corporate Acquisitions: Specific Case of Management Buyouts and Leveraged Buyouts

4.7.1. Scope of MBOs and LBOs

The yet largely unregulated corporate financing schemes of Management Buyouts (MBO) and Leveraged Buyouts (LBO) consist of the acquisition of a financially troubled yet economically viable company within:

a) A financial consolidation contract, concluded by a financially troubled company and credit institutions and other interested partners. The objective is to improve the company's financial status by rescheduling debts, granting additional financing or increasing the share capital;

b)   A corporate restructuring contract, concluded by the abovementioned parties, but having the objective of recovering the company's profitability by restructuring it through the disposal of company's assets or businesses, the change of its legal status, or its merger or splitting.

MBO's and LBO's are regulated by Decree-Law 81/98 of 2nd April 1998, and the abovementioned contracts are overseen by the *Instituto Português de Apoio às Pequenas e Médias Empresas e ao Investimento* (the Portuguese public institute that is responsible for the promotion of small and medium-sized enterprises).

4.7.2. Acquirers

MBOs under Decree-Law 41/98 are promoted by company managers, whether connected to the company or not, or by company employees. This Decree-Law contains no requirements for the company which will serve as vehicle for the MBO, i.e., that will formally acquire or merge with the company targeted by the MBO. Typically, the former is created solely for the purposes of the MBO. In that case, it should be incorporated as a pure holding company (*Sociedade Gestora de Participações Sociais - SGPS*) under Decree-Law 495/88, as amended, since only such companies can have the acquisition and management of holdings in other companies as their corporate object.

4.7.3. Financial Leverage

The financial leverage of MBOs carried out under Decree-Law 81/98 is not regulated but is nonetheless implicitly referred to by Decree-Law 41/98, since it states that the target company may assume the debt incurred by its managers in the acquisition procedures, provided that the amount of such debt is expressly mentioned in the financial consolidation contract and that it is approved by a special shareholders meeting resolution approved by at least a 75% majority of voting shareholders.

4.7.4. MBOs of Public Companies

MBOs of public companies require a takeover bid, to be carried out on the Stock Exchange in accordance with Securities Code requirements on takeover bids and previously registered with the Stock Market Supervisory Authority (*Comissão de Mercado de Valores Mobiliários* "CMVM").

COMPETITION AND ANTITRUST LAW

CHAPTER 5

5.1. Introduction

From the mid-1980s the Portuguese economy ended profound changes as a result of the liberalisation, deregulation and opening to the private sector of key areas of economic activity as well as of the advances in political, economic and monetary integration of the European Union, which Portugal joined in 1986. The country thus became more attractive to foreign and domestic investors and increased its potential for growth. From that point on, the Portuguese provisions on competition were introduced in the context of the European Union legal framework.

5.2. European Union Legal Framework

One of the main goals of the European Union is to ensure effective competition between companies operating in its territory, thus allowing them to carry out their activities as if they were doing so within the borders of a national market.

The European Union Treaty, as revised by the Treaty of Nice (in force since 2002), provides the Member States with a "system ensuring that competition can not be distorted in the European internal market" since it would be difficult, if not impossible, for individual Member States to achieve this goal through the use of their national policies and legislation alone. Moreover, "the promotion of a high degree of competitiveness and convergence of economic performance" is one of the fundamental objectives of the European Community.

The Treaty prohibits any cartel or restrictive practice that impairs the existence of effective competition in the common market. Thus, all agreements between companies, decisions by associations of companies and concerted practices which may affect trade between Member States, and which have the goal or the result of preventing, restricting or distorting competition are prohibited unless they comply with any of the criteria laid out in number 3 of article 81. This notion of cartels or restrictive practices excludes those agreements that may be considered of minor importance (under the terms of Commission Regulation 2001/C 368/07) as well as those which prove to be economically advantageous, following an evaluation of the balance between their costs and benefits.

The Treaty also prohibits the abuse of a dominant position in the common market. No company may carry out its activities mistreating its suppliers, distributors, consumers or competitors, immune from the regular constraints of a competitive market. The article goes on to provide a list of examples such as unfair pricing or restrictive tie-in agreements.

Although the Treaty does not forbid state aid, it does subject it to the control of such community principles as the rule of non-discrimination. Therefore, aid may not be granted in a manner, which distorts or threatens to distort competition within the common market by favouring certain companies or the production of certain goods.

The enforcement of these provisions is regulated by a number of legislative acts such as:
- Regulation 1/2003 of the Council (16/12/2002);
- Communication 2001/C 368/07 (22/12/2001) of the Commission, that contains the notion of agreements of minor importance which do not fall under the scope of the legal prohibitions;
- Communication 97/C 372/03 of the Commission (09/12/1997), which better explains the concept of relevant market for the purpose of the prohibition contained in the Treaty; A

relevant market comprises a product or group of products and the geographic area in which these products are produced and/or traded. Therefore, the relevant market has two components: the product market and the geographic market.

- Regulation 4064/89 of the Council (21/12/1989), last amended by Regulation 1310/97 (30/6/1997), concerning the control of mergers.

5.3. Portuguese Legal Framework

Amongst the state's essential social and economic responsibilities is the one relating directly to the subject of competition: "ensuring an effective operation of the markets, in order to guarantee balanced competition between companies, to prevent the existence of monopolies and to restrain the abuse of dominant positions and any other practices that may harm the general interest" (article 81/e) of the Portuguese Constitution).

Competition was first addressed by Decree-Law 422/83 of 3rd December 1983, with regard to the destructive economic effects flowing from agreements and practices agreed upon between companies, decisions of professional associations and from the abuse of a dominant market position as well as to individual practices deemed to be anticompetitive.

Decree-Law 422/83 was then repealed by Decree-Law 371/93 of 29th October 1993, which established a general legal framework for defending and promoting competition in order to achieve the goal set by article 81, e) of the Portuguese Constitution.

By doing so, it also introduced innovations, one of which was the regulation of practices that may distort competition, mergers and acquisitions and state aid, in direct relation with the relevant European Union provisions. Another innovation was addressing the abuse of economic dependence even when it was practised by companies without a dominant position in the market.

This framework also included a set of procedural and institutional provisions, the latter having been most recently replaced by Decree-Law 10/2003 of 18 January.

Meanwhile, Decree-Laws 370/93 of 29th October 1993 and 253/86 of 25th August 1986, both amended by Decree-Law 140/98 of 16th May 1998, regulate individual commercial practices, promotional and low-priced sales respectively.

5.4. Competition Authority

After 20 years of experience with the enforcement of Decree-Law 371/93, as well as previous legislation, the need was felt to create a single and independent authority that would replace both the Competition Council (*Conselho da Concorrência*) and the Directorate-General for Commerce and Competition (*Direcção-Geral do Comércio e da Concorrência*) in the role of a supervisory authority for competition matters (a task that was assigned to them by Decree-Law 371/93).

Decree-Law 10/2003 created the Competition Authority (*Autoridade da Concorrência*), which also aimed to replace the remaining material and procedural provisions of Decree-Law

371/93 in accordance with the most recent reform of European Union Legislation on competition as quickly as possible.

The Competition Authority is empowered to:

i) Ensure compliance with competition regulations, laws and decisions;

ii) Survey, in a systematic manner, commercial and distribution activities and monitor market indicators, so as to evaluate the impact of sectorial policies, at the request of the minister responsible for economic matters;

iii) Execute any competence assigned to national administrative authorities by European Community Law;

iv) Ensure the technical representation of Portugal in any European Community or International bodies in the matters of competition;

iv) Identifying and investigating any restrictive practices and, when identified, imposing legal sanctions;

v)   Taking precautionary measures, when needed;

vi) Deciding on any administrative procedures relating to mergers and acquisitions that are subject to prior notification;

vii) Approving or proposing new regulations on competition as well as codes of conduct for companies, and issuing recommendations and general directives.

Decisions on imposing fines for infringement of competition law taken by the Competition Authority can be challenged in the Lisbon Commercial Court.

5.5. Main Areas Covered by Portuguese Competition Law

5.5.1. Restrictive Practices

Decree-Law 371/93 prohibits all restrictive practices (i.e., agreements between companies or groups of companies, decisions by associations of companies and concerted practices), which may prevent, restrict or distort competition within Portugal, namely those relating to:

a) Fixing prices and/or other sales conditions;

b) Output restrictions as regards production, distribution, research and development, or investment;

c) Market share allocation;

d) Discriminatory sales prices or conditions;

e) Group boycotts;

f) Imposition of additional disparate obligations as *sine qua non* conditions for the conclusion of a contract.

However, certain practices, which contribute to improving the production or distribution of goods or services, or to promoting technical or economic progress may be considered justified, provided that they:

i)   Allow consumers a fair share of the resulting benefit;

ii)   Do not impose restrictions on the companies involved, which are not fundamental to the attainment of these objectives; and

iii) Do not allow those companies the possibility of eliminating competition in respect of a substantial part of the goods and services in question.

Such an exemption from the abovementioned prohibition is granted by the Competition Authority at the request of the companies concerned.

5.5.2. Abuse of an Economic Dependence

Abuse of a dominant position in the market by one or more companies is forbidden. A company, or group of companies, is deemed to hold a dominant position where (a) a sole company holds a market share of 30% or higher, (b) two or three companies hold a combined market share equal to, or greater than, 50%, (c) four or five companies hold a combined market share equal to, or greater than 70%. Abusive behaviour may consist of any of the infringements listed in paragraph 1 of item 5.5.1.

Also prohibited is the abuse of economic dependence. For the purposes of Decree-Law 371/93, a company is deemed to depend economically on another where it is obliged to rely on the latter as a client or supplier lacking a comparable alternative. Abusive kinds of behaviour may also consist of any of those listed in paragraph 1 of item 5.5.1.

5.5.3. Mergers and Acquisitions

Certain merger and acquisition operations may be deemed anticompetitive as they lead to concentrations of companies, which may offset market balance to the detriment of smaller companies.

Therefore, prior approval by the Competition Authority is required for such operations wherever:

i)   They result in a 30% or higher share in the market for specific goods or services, or in a substantial part thereof; or

ii)   The combined turnover (net of tax) of companies concerned, in the year prior to that of the operation in question, exceeded EUR 150,000,000.

This requirement does not apply to credit institutions, financial companies or insurance companies. Operations subject to this requirement include:

(i) Mergers;

(ii) Acquisition, by a company, of the totality of another company's share capital, or of a controlling participation thereon, or of rights granting the former a predominant influence over the composition of the latter's corporate bodies or over the resolutions passed by such bodies;

(iii) Acquisition, by a company, of the totality or of a substantial part of another company's assets;

(iv) Constitution, by two or more companies, of a common company, under whatever form, if it is of a lasting nature and does not have as objective the coordination of competition between the founding companies or between them and the common undertaking.

Cross-border merger or acquisition operations must comply with Commission Regulation (EC) 4064/89, referred to above, including the duty to notify the Commission.

5.5.4. State Aid

Aid granted by the state or other entities governed by public law is also prohibited where it restricts or affects competition in a significant manner. This prohibition aims to maintain balanced competition within the Portuguese market by preventing protectionist measures leading to the emergence of monopolies and oligopolies capable of imposing prices and/or other conditions to the detriment of consumers.

Compensations awarded by the state, under whatever form, in exchange for the supply of a public service or under Government or Parliament approved development programmes are excluded from the notion of State aid.

This prohibition does not apply to horizontal state aid, i.e. specific cross-industry rules for particular categories of aid which reach all economic sectors, approved by the Commission under the EC Treaty and under Council Regulation (EC) 994/98 of 7th May 1998, referred to above.

5.5.5. Individual Practices

Certain practices between individual merchants, such as imposing dissimilar purchase or selling prices or other unfair trading conditions, dumping, or refusing to provide services, as well as reduced-prices sales are also restricted and/or regulated by Decree-Laws 370/93 of 29th October 1993 and Decree-Law 253/86 of 25th August 1986, respectively. Although not likely to distort the market severely, these individual practices or reduced-price sales may seriously affect market transparency and therefore market efficiency.

Thus, when carried out between individual merchants, discriminatory pricing, boycotts (even if the boycotted good is non-essential and market supply is not affected) or the imposition of pricing, payment or sales conditions disproportionate to the benefit resulting from the sale or from the supply of services, are forbidden. Nonetheless, boycotts may be considered justified under certain circumstances, e.g., the need by the vendor to ensure the fulfilment of obligations previously assumed or a stock for self-consumption or security purposes, the inability of the acquirer to ensure a resale under proper technical conditions, and/or default by the acquirer on the payment of previous orders.

Meanwhile, reduced-price sales (i.e., promotional sales, end-of-season sales or on sale operations) are only allowed if intended for advertising a new product, increasing sales volume or hastening product outflow. Price reductions (including information on both the new and old prices) must be properly disclosed to consumers as well as the date of the beginning and duration of the promotional period.

5.6. Sanctions and Penalties

Infringements to competition law are punished through administrative fines imposed by the Competition Authority, notwithstanding the criminal liability eventually incurred by the offender. Infringements to the prohibition of restrictive practices are punished with a fine of between EUR 498.80 and EUR 997,595.79.

Administrative fines are enforced, or challenged before the Courts, in accordance with a simplified and expeditious system applying sanctions to administrative offences, rather than the burdensome procedures applying to criminal offences. Such a system was introduced by Decree-Law 433/82 of 27th October 1982, as amended by Decree-Laws 356/89 of 17th October 1989, 244/95 of 14th September 1995, 323/2001 of 17th December 2001 and by Law 109/2001 of 24th December 2001.

Although sometimes additional sanctions may be imposed on offenders, such as the seizure of the offender's assets or temporary suspension of any authorisation or license granted to the offender, Decree-Law 371/93 does not impose additional sanctions cn infringements of competition law, other than administrative fines, except for the nullity of contracts concluded in breach of a decision refusing the approval of, or setting out certain conditions for, a merger or acquisition subject to such an approval, as referred to in item 5.5.3. above.

CONSUMER PROTECTION
CHAPTER 6

6.1. Introduction

Consumer policy involves the development of legislative initiatives, to empower consumers by enhancing the role of consumer representatives in decision-making. It is essential that the Portuguese government addresses consumer concerns in all its policies aimed at protecting the interests, health and safety of consumers in the Portuguese market.

At constitutional level these aims are enshrined in article 60 of the 1976 Constitution of the Republic of Portugal, last revised in 2001, which identifies basic rights as regards consumer protection in relation to goods and services, health, safety and economic interests, as well as to redress.

6.2. European Legal Framework

The key European provisions regarding the legal framework for consumer protection:

- Council Directive 85/374/EEC of 25th July 1985 as amended by Directive 1999/34/EC of the European Parliament and of the Council of 10th May 1999 on liability for defective products;

- Directive 84/450/EC of 10th September 1984 on misleading advertising, as amended by the European Parliament and of the Council Directive 97/55/EC of the of 6th October 1997 on comparative advertising;

- Council Directive 93/13/EEC of 5th April 1993 on unfair terms in consumer contracts;

- European Parliament and Council Directive 2001/95/EC of 3rd December 2001 on general product safety;

- Council Directive 87/577/EC of 20th December 1985 on the protection of the consumer in respect of contracts negotiated away from places of business ("the doorstep selling directive");

- Council Directive 87/102/EEC of 22nd December 1986 for the approximation of the laws, regulations and administrative provisions of the Member States concerning consumer credit as amended by Council Directive 90/88/EEC of 22nd February 1990 and European Parliament and Council Directive 98/7/EC of 16th February 1998;

- Directive 97/7/EC of the European Parliament and of the Council of 20th May 1997 on the protection of consumers in respect of distance contracts[1];

---

[1] In the UK, a distance contract is defined by The Consumer Protection (Distance Selling) Regulations 2000, which incorporated the EU Directive, as "any contract concerning goods and

- European Commission's Directive 98/6/EC on price indications;

- Directive 2000/31/EC of the European Parliament and of the Council of 8th June 2000 on legal aspects of information society services ("the electronic commerce directive").

6.3. Portuguese Consumer Law

6.3.1. The Legal Framework for Consumer Protection

The legal framework for consumer protection in Portugal was first introduced by Law 29/81 of 22nd August 1981, which also established the *Instituto Nacional de Defesa do Consumidor* (National Institute for Consumer Protection), a legal entity governed by public law serving as the supervisory authority for consumer affairs, renamed *Instituto do Consumidor* (Consumer Institute - IC) by Decree-Law 195/93 of 24th May 1993, which also laid down the IC's assignments and powers, including that of imposing penalties and fines where required by law.

Law 24/96 of 31st July 1996, which replaced Law 29/81and the new Decree-Law 67/03 of 8th April gave consumer protection a new impetus, since it enlarged and clarified the scope of consumer rights, in line with EU consumer policy, while the IC was granted new powers and the capacity to enforce consumer rights and the collective interests of consumers. Nowadays the IC is highly respected and looked upon as a pre-eminent authority whenever consumer rights are involved.

Information on the plethora of decisions, regulations and directives that apply to consumption in Europe is now available for consumers in consumer advice centres (info-centres), created to help them avoid the many pitfalls laid down by such legislation, such as the *(Centros de Informação Autárquicos ao Consumidor* - C.I.A.C)* or *Serviços Municipais de Informação ao Consumidor* (Consumer Information Municipal Centres – S.M.I.C.), which provide free information services to consumers at a municipal level.

Furthermore, extra-judicial resolution of consumer disputes is now possible through a network of arbitration centres spread all over the country, some of which are directly subordinated to the I.C.

---

services concluded between the supplier and the consumer under an organised distance sales or service-provision scheme run by the supplier who, for the purpose of the contract, makes exclusive use of one or more means of distance communication up to and including the moment at which the contract is concluded"

6.3.2. Sectoral Legislation

Sectoral consumer protection is also ensured by a vast body of legislation, a sample of which is listed below and is a clear demonstration of the growth of consumer protection requirements in direct proportion to that of market complexity and of consumer demand.

6.3.2.1. Consumer Contracts

- Articles 397 to 1250 of the Portuguese Civil Code, as approved by Decree-Law 47 344 of 25th November 1966, laying down common provisions on contracts;
- Decree Law 446/85 of 25th October 1985, as amended by Decree-Law 220/95 of 31st January 1995 and Decree-Law 249/99 of 7th July 1999, implementing the legal framework for general agreement clauses as well as Council Directive 93/13/EEC of 5th April 1993 on unfair terms in consumer contracts, i.e., the contracts concluded between the seller of goods or supplier of services on the one hand, and the consumer on the other hand.

6.3.2.2. Consumer Credit

- Decree-Law 359/91 of 21st September 1991, as amended by Decree-Law 101/2000 of 2nd June 2000, providing for the legal framework for consumer credit and implementing Council Directive 87/102/EEC of 22nd December 1987, for the approximation of the laws, regulations and administrative provisions of the Member States concerning consumer credit, as amended by Council Directive 90/88/EEC of 22nd February 1990 and Directive 98/7/EC of the Council and of the European Parliament of 16th February 1998.

6.3.2.3. Trade

- Decree-Law 383/89 of 6th November 1989, as amended by Decree-Law 131/2001 of 24th April 2001, on liability for defective products, implementing Council Directive 85/374, of 25th July 1985, on the approximation of the laws, regulations and administrative provisions of the Member States concerning liability for defective products, as amended by Directive 1999/34/EC of the European Parliament and of the Council of 10th May 1999.
- Decree Laws 296/98 of 25th September 1998 and 206/99 of 25th May 1999, laying down the legal framework and standards for the quality, packaging, labelling, marketing and advertising of beauty and hygienic products and implementing Council Directive 93/35/EEC of 14th June 1993, and Commission Directive 95/17/EC of 19th June 1995;

- Decree-Law 143/2001 of 26th April 2001, implementing Directive 97/7/EC of the European Parliament and of the Council of 20th May 1997 on the protection of consumers in respect of distance contracts;

- Resolution of the Council of Ministers 115/98 of 6th August 1998 creating the National Initiative for E-Commerce;

- Resolution of the Council of Ministers 94/99 of 25th August 1999 laying down the guidelines for the National Initiative for E-Commerce;

- Decree-Law 290-D/99 of 2nd August 1999 and Decree-Law 62/2003 of 3 rd april (that implements the European Parliament and Council directive 1999/93/CE of 13th December) laying out the legal framework for the issuance and verification of electronic invoices and digital signatures;

- Decree-Law 375/99 of 18th September 1999 equating electronic invoices to paper-based invoices for the purposes of verification of the former within legal proceedings;

- Decree Law 354/86 of 23rd October 1986, as amended by Decree-Law 373/90 of 27 November 1990 and by Decree-Law 44/92 of 31st March 1992, laying down the legal framework for the activity of renting cars without drivers;

- Decree-Law 251/98 of 11th August 1998, as amended by Law 156/99 of 14th September 1999 and by Law 106/2001 of 31st August 2001, and Decree Law 297/92 of 31st December 1992, laying down the legal framework for the access to and pursuit of the provision as well as the pricing of passenger transportation services in taxis.

6.3.2.4. Competition and Advertising

- The Portuguese Advertising Code (*Código da Publicidade*), as approved by Decree-Law 330/90 of 23rd October and as amended by Decree-Laws 74/93 of 10th March 1993, 6/95 of 17th January 1995, 61/97 of 25th March 1997 and 332/2001 of 24th December 2001, laying down the legal framework for advertising, pursuant to which all advertising must comply with the principles of (1) Lawfulness (*contra bonos mores*), (2) Identifiableness of the advertising message, (3) Accuracy of the advertising message and (4) respect for consumer rights;

- Decree-Law 370/93 of 29th October 1993, as amended by Decree-Law 140/98 of 16 May 1998, prohibiting certain commercial practices;

- Decree-Law 371/93 of 29th October 1993, and Governmental Order (Portaria) 1097/93 of 29th October, laying down the legal framework for competition.

6.3.2.5. Protection of Personal Data

- Law 67/98 of 26th October 1998 implementing Directive 95/46/EC of the European Parliament and of the Council of 24th October 1995 on the protection of individuals with regard to the processing of personal data and on the free movement of such data;

- Law 69/98 of 28th October 1998 implementing Directive 97/66/EC of the European Parliament and of the Council of 15th December 1997 concerning the processing of personal data and the protection of privacy in the telecommunications sector.

6.3.2.6. Resolution of Consumer Disputes and Legal Aid

- Law 21/86 of 29th August 1986 laying down the procedures for resolution of disputes by means of voluntary arbitration courts;

- Decree-Law 146/99 of 4th May 1999 laying down the procedures for the extra-judicial resolution of consumer disputes;

- Governmental Order (*Portaria*) 81/2001 of 8th February 2001, as amended by Governmental Order (*Portaria*) 350/2001 of 9th April 2001, providing for an updated list of entities allowed to resolve disputes through arbitration procedures;

- Law 30-E/2000 of 20th December 2000 laying out the legal framework for access to legal aid schemes.

CONVEYANCING

CHAPTER 7

7.1. Introduction

Conveyancing is substantially more complex in Portugal than in common law countries, given the many steps involved in the transfer of the ownership of property through a sale and purchase, as well as urban construction and land subdivision, for construction purposes. This chapter addresses the most relevant aspects.

7.2. Legal Framework

The key provisions regarding real estate property are contained in:

(i) The Portuguese Civil Code, in particular articles 202 to 216 and 1344 to 1402 thereof;

(ii) Decree-Law 555/99, of 16th December 1999, as amended by Decree-Law 177/2001 of 4th June 2001, which codifies rules on (a) the subdivision of green field sites for the purposes of construction (b) permits for constructing, modifying or restoring buildings (c) licensing buildings or parts thereof for residential or non-residential use;

(iii) Decree-Law 281/99 of 26th July 1999, requiring notaries public to verify, before executing a deed of purchase concerning a building or a part thereof, that a valid construction or inhabitation license for such a building or part thereof exists or has been applied for;

(iv) Decree-Law 380/99 of 22nd September 1999 as amended by Decree-law 53/2000 of 7th April of 2000, containing the legal framework for national, regional and local land management and urban planning;

(v) Decree-Laws 384/88 of 25th October 1988 and 103/90 of 22nd March 1990, relating to land consolidation through reparcelling of farmland plots.

7.3. Definition of Green Field Sites and Urban Property

The Portuguese Civil Code differentiates between green field sites and urban property. Article 204 (2) thereof defines a green field site as a *"confined portion of land, as well as the existing constructions on it which do not have economic autonomy"*, and urban property as *"all the structures erected on the soil, as well as the land that surrounds the building"*.

A given property serves as a green field site or as an urban property in accordance with the use it is given by its proprietor and with state land management and urban planning policies. In particular,

104

such policies are essential in determining whether a green field site can be converted into urban property.

Thus, in evaluating a given property, not only its geographical location and size but also and most especially land management and urban planning instruments should be taken into consideration.

Furthermore, under Decree-Law 380/99 of 22nd September 1999, referred to above, interested parties are entitled to gather information on land management and urban planning from the state or regional or local authorities, and under Decree-Law 555/99 of 16th December 1999 interested parties may request from Municipalities preliminary information on the feasibility of a given urban development (building construction, demolition or repair, land subdivision, etc.). Thus, such authorities are obliged to disclose information about the limitations and restrictions, which may apply to a given property.

7.4. Property Subdivision for Construction Purposes

No subdivision of land property for construction purposes can take place without prior permission granted by the City Council ("*Câmara Municipal*") or authorisation granted by the Mayor ("*Presidente da Câmara Municipal*").

Permission granted by the City Council is only required where the subdivision relates to one or more properties located in an area not covered by a Council approved development plan (*plano de pormenor*), while authorisation granted by the Mayor applies wherever such property or properties are located in an area already covered by an approved development plan (*plano de pormenor*).

Subdivision licensing procedures include public discussion of the subdivision project (which can be dispensed with if the project relates to a small-size property) and consultation with external departments (e.g., the Environment Ministry) where legally required. Neither of these procedures is required in subdivision authorisation procedures.

Once this license or authorisation is granted, the proprietor may either submit construction plans or sell the property *en bloc* together with the benefit of the subdivision license, or sell each individual plot resulting from the subdivision separately.

7.5. License or Authorisation to Build, Modify, or Demolish a Building

Construction of a building or modification or demolition thereof can only take place under a license or authorisation granted by the City Council or the Mayor. However, this license or authorisation is not required for modifications to the inside of a building or part thereof, provided that they do not entail any modification to the building's main structure, roofing or façade.

The application for an authorisation or a license for constructing, modifying or demolishing a building must include an architectural plan as well as all additional legally required plans (which can be delivered no later than six months after the approval of the architectural plan). However, where the application relates to a license for constructing or modifying a building located in an area not covered by a development plan (*plano de pormenor*), a partial license for structure construction may be granted upon approval of the architectural plan and delivery of the additional legally required plans.

Where a license or authorisation for construction, modification or demolition of a building or part thereof was applied for on behalf of a specific person or entity and this person or entity transfers ownership of the building, or of the property where it is to be constructed, to a third person, a modification to the application must be requested, so that the license or authorisation is issued to the new owner.

Upon the issuance of a license or authorisation for constructing or modifying a building, supply of utilities such as water, electricity, telephone lines, sewerage amongst others can be applied for.

7.6. Promissory Contract for the Purchase of Property

Promissory contracts for the purchase and sale of property are widely used within conveyancing in Portugal. The main features of promissory contracts in Portugal are laid out below.

7.6.1. Recommendations

Before entering into negotiations regarding a promissory contract for the purchase of a property, certain enquiries are recommended.

Properties, as well as all facts pertaining to the ownership of such assets, must be registered with the relevant Land Registry (*Conservatória do Registo Predial*). Thus, the actual ownership of the property (as well as the existence of any mortgage) can be verified through an updated certificate issued by the Land Registry.

Gathering information on the tax assessment of the property in question is also recommended. This can be done through a certificate issued by the Local Tax Department (*Repartição de Finanças*) with jurisdiction over the area in which the asset is located.

7.6.2. Requirements

The key rules relating to formalities of promissory contracts are the following:
(i) The promissory contract must be made in writing, whenever the final contract must be made in writing or through a notarial deed (the latter case being that of the purchase or sale of a property), signed by the promisor, or by both parties where the promisee is binding for both parties;
(ii) Where the final contract concerns the purchase of, or the constitution of a right *in rem* over a building or part thereof, either existing or under construction or to be constructed, a notary public must certify the signatures of the parties and verify the existence of a utilisation permit or a valid authorisation or license for the construction of the building.

Promissory contracts are also subject to specific enforcement regulations. In fact, unless there is a deposit or a penalty clause, if the promissory contract is breached by a party, the other party may enforce the contract through a court order under which the final contract becomes fully executable notwithstanding the default on the promissory contract.

7.6.3. Deposit (*"Sinal"*)
The parties can agree that, upon concluding a promissory contract for the purchase of a given property, the promisor (purchaser) shall give the promisee (seller) a deposit (*sinal*) - usually an amount of money -, which serves as a first instalment or may also serve as a penalty clause. In the event of default on the promissory contract, imputable to the promisor, the deposit becomes the property of the promisee. Conversely, if the breach of contract is attributable to the promisee (seller), the promisor (purchaser) is entitled to demand an amount double the one he paid by way of deposit.

7.7. Real Estate Property Purchase Contracts

The Portuguese Civil Code defines a purchase contract as one through which one person's property rights on a given asset are transferred to another person against monetary consideration.

In the following sections some of the legal requirements, which apply to contracts for the purchase of green field sites, subdivided property, property under construction and of urban property are highlighted.

7.8. Requirements for the Purchase of Green Field Sites, Subdivided Property, Property Under Construction and Urban Property

7.8.1. Common Requirements

7.8.1.1. Form of Purchase Contract

A purchase contract of a property must be made by means of a notarial deed and the notary public will not sign and seal this deed unless the necessary legal requirements have been satisfied.

7.8.1.2. Documentation to be filed with the Notary Public

The following documentation must be filed with the notary public prior to the execution of the deed:

i) Registration certificate issued by the Land Registry (*Conservatória do Registo Predial*);

ii) Tax Department certificate (*Caderneta Predial*) – a stamp provided by the Tax Department confirming the property's tax status. The stamp is valid for 12 months and can be renewed. If the property has not been registered with the tax department, a duplicate of the registration application is required, stamped by the tax department;

iii) Receipt for payment of "tax on the transfer of real estate properties" ("*IMT*"). Assessment of this tax must be requested by the purchaser at the competent Tax Department and paid before the transfer takes place. The *IMT* is levied on the value of the property in accordance with the tax rates indicated in chapter 13, section 7, of this Guide.

7.8.1.3. Registration of Contract with the Land Registry ("*Conservatória do Registo Predial*")

Transfer of property rights to the purchaser is only completed upon the registration of the purchase and sale contract with the Land Registration Office.

7.8.2. Specific Requirements for the Purchase of Green Field Sites

There are no specific requirements with regard to the purchase of green field sites other than those laid out in item 7.8.1. above.

7.8.3. Specific Requirements for the Purchase of Subdivided Property

The requirements are the same as those laid out in item 7.8.1. above. However, the property subdivision license or authorisation must be presented to the notary public upon the execution of the deed of purchase and sale.

7.8.4. Specific Requirements for the Purchase of Property Under Construction

The requirements are the same as those laid out in item 7.8.1. above. However, a valid construction license or authorisation must be presented to the notary public upon the execution of the deed of purchase and sale.

7.8.5. Specific Requirements for the Purchase of Urban Property

7.8.5.1. Form of Contract

As stated above a notarial deed is required for the purchase of urban property. However if the purchase is for residential purposes only and transacted with recourse to a bank loan, the notarial deed can be replaced by a private document based on a Government-approved model, the parties' signatures being certified by a notary public.

7.8.5.2. Permission to Use a Building ("*Licença de Utilização*")

In addition to the requirements laid out in item 7.8.1. above, a notarial deed relating to the purchase of a building or part thereof will only be executed if the notary public verifies that the said building or part thereof is registered with the Tax Department and that permission to use was granted by the municipal authorities. Such permission is granted by the Mayor and certifies the conformity of the building or part thereof with the specifications contained in the construction license or permission.

In regard to newly constructed buildings, in relation to which permission to use has not yet been granted, the latter can be replaced by the construction authorisation or license, provided that:

i)   The transferor is able to prove that he has already applied for permission to use the building or part thereof;

ii)   The transferor states that (a) the construction has been completed, (b) neither was the construction embargoed by municipal authorities nor the construction license withdrawn, and (c) the abovementioned permission was applied for more than 50 days before and the applicant is yet to be notified of any response to the application.

CORPORATE GOVERNANCE
CHAPTER 8

Sir Adrian Cadbury, where defining that corporate governance consists of "the system whereby companies are directed and controlled", sets out the basic principles from which stems the definition of corporate governance adopted by the Stock Market Supervisory Authority (*Comissão de Mercado de Valores Mobiliários*, hereinafter "CMVM"). This criteria underpins the recommendations and binding rules on Corporate Governance issued by CMVM.

In a country like Portugal, which has a small stock market, only a limited number of companies with more than half of their share capital in free-float, and where the free trade in shares as well as the shareholders' assessment of the management bodies' performance are impaired by the existence of defensive mechanisms such as golden shares or capped voting rights, it is fundamental that such a legal and regulatory framework encourages companies to raise their standards of management, aligning themselves with those of most European countries, in accordance with the principle of transparency. The momentum is for maximising shareholder value, fostering shareholder activism and rendering boards accountable in their management of companies.

The growing media and public interest in governance issues, in light of recent corporate scandals, in particular investors concerns with corporate governance practices and the need for transparency in corporate management, has forced authorities to develop and reform the legal framework in order to adjust it to market changes, globalisation and the internationalisation of companies.

The European Commission presented an Action Plan on corporate governance in May 2003 focused on the requirement to disclose information by boards and on an increase in shareholders' influence over the company. The European Union is also set on limiting the ability of national governments and companies to obstruct international take-over operations that may result in the transfer of decision centres to other countries. This Action Plan is composed of a number of different proposals, and the one related specifically to corporate governance was defined as a priority (2003-2005).

In Portugal, the CMVM (*Comissão de Mercado de Valores Mobiliários*, the Stock Market Supervisory Authority) also updated its recommendations and regulations on these matters in 2003, amending CMVM Regulations 11/2000 and 7/2001 and the CMVM Recommendations on corporate governance through regulation 11/2003. The main goal is to raise the regulatory standard applied to domestic companies, in order to align their corporate governance practices with other European countries, thus restoring investors' trust in the Portuguese stock market.

And so, the guidelines of these reforms are mainly focused on strengthening disclosure and information duties, setting up requirements in respect of the "independence of directors", of remuneration packages and remuneration policies, as well as, reinforcing mechanisms to ensure independence and transparency.

In fact, the Portuguese legal and regulatory framework on corporate governance includes not only regulations and non-binding recommendations from the CMVM, but also specific legal provisions from the Portuguese Companies Code and the Portuguese Securities Code. Provisions from the Companies Code and the Securities Code, as well as regulations from CMVM, are mandatory. However, even CMVM recommendations (as opposed to mandatory regulations) gain binding force given the requirement stated in Regulation 7/2001, as amended. according to which, all companies must disclose, in a annual report on corporate governance, which recommendations they apply and which they do not apply, and also justify every non-compliance.

The provisions on corporate governance, are primarily aimed at publicly traded companies, but they may also play an important role in setting standards for corporate governance in private or state-owned companies.

The main issues covered by these provisions are the following:

8.1. – Disclosure of Information and Transparency

8.1.1. – Independence Criteria

8.1.2. – The Annual Report on Corporate Governance Compliance

8.2. – Exercise of Shareholder Rights

8.2.1. Exercise of Shareholder Voting and Representation Rights

8.2.2. Exercise of Minority Shareholders' Rights

8.3. – Defensive Devices Against Takeover Bids

8.4. – Composition of the Board

8.4.1. - Remuneration Policy

8.5. – Institutional Investors

8.1. Disclosure of Information and Transparency

According to both the CMVM recommendations and regulations, companies must disclose information on preparatory documents for general meetings and financial information, through the use of new technologies. The use of new technologies for the disclosure of information has been added to Regulation 7/2001, as amended, in its new article 3A, now making it a mandatory provision.

Besides these recommendations, article 289 of the Portuguese Companies Code also stipulates that, preparatory information must be made available to shareholders 15 days before general meetings and article 290 specifies shareholders' rights to information concerning subjects that are being discussed in a general meeting.

CMVM Recommendations, also advise the implementation of measures that should help create equal access to information for all shareholders. Recommendations I/1 and III/3 advise the creation of an internal system for risk control, which should also promote the disclosure of information on the matter of assessment of risks inherent to the company's activities.

The IV/9 Recommendation of the 2003 CMVM that amended Recommendations on corporate governance, adds a new and important provision, advising the disclosure of the remuneration of each board member.

Along with all this information, article 2 of Regulation 7/2001, as amended, also stipulates that all information related to plans for the allotment of shares and/or stock options to employees and/or members of the board of directors must be submitted to the CMVM.

According to article 3/1 of Regulation 7/2001, as amended, the CMVM must be informed of the acquisition and disposal of shares issued by a company, by the members of the board of directors of that company or of its parent company. They are also required under, article 3/4, to disclose the number of shares held by that company and the percentage of voting rights attributable to them under the terms of article 20 of the Portuguese Securities Code. However, Regulation 7/2001, as amended, now states that this information must be provided to the held company, which must then disclose it to the CMVM, as opposed to being directly disclosed to the CMVM.

The same provision states that, this information must be provided within 7 working days of the transaction and/or allocation relevant, which, in case of an operation of issuing shares, is the signing of the public deed.

Article 3A of the amended Regulation 7/2001, requires that all the information listed in this provision (for example, data mentioned in article 171 of the Companies Code, such as corporate name or head office) be made accessible, through the Internet, with the requisites herein described. In this way, all listed companies are now obliged to maintain a website where all this information is made available and are no longer only "advised" to do so by a non-binding recommendation.

Article 1 of Regulation 7/2001, as amended, stipulates an obligation to disclose information concerning the level of compliance with the CMVM recommendations in an annual report, which must include the structure and management of the company, in compliance with the high quality standards demanded by article 7 of the Portuguese Securities Code (a reference to this same provision of the Securities Code was made in the Annex to Regulation 7/2001 as amended, paragraph 1).

8.1.1. Independence Criteria

It is recommended, that the board also includes a number of independent directors.

Their role is important in representing the interests of minority shareholders and in overseeing executive directors in financial areas and areas that affect the strategy and future of the company, as well as, areas where executive directors may have conflicts of interest.

It is worth mentioning, that Portuguese boards tend to differentiate between non-executive and independent directors, and to include a certain number of both. Non-executive directors can be independent or not and this definition of 'independence' is linked to the non-representation of dominant shareholders of the company.

We have recently witnessed the appointment of non-executive directors who represent one or more minority shareholders.

Independent and non-executive directors have an important role to play in appointment committees, remuneration committees and audit boards.

Ideally, the majority of non-executive directors should be independent, not only from shareholders, but also from any operational business of the company.

Finally, and in line with CMVM, the appointment of independent executive directors is also recommended, in order to prevent corporate decisions from being taken in the interests of dominant of shareholders alone and to ensure that the best interests of the company are preserved.

Regulation 7/2001 as amended by regulation 11/2003 sets out a certain criteria for determination of the independence of the board members. The criteria lists those who cannot be considered independent directors:

a) members of the board holding cross-directorships;

b) members of the board holding qualified shareholdings of at least 10% of the company's share capital or voting rights;

c) members of the board who are employed or carry out duties of administration in a competing company;

d) members of the board earning remunerations from the company, except for the remuneration earned when carrying out duties of management;

e) members of the board who are married or have close family ties with any of the abovementioned individuals;

Therefore, it must be verified that each director has no material relationship with the company (directly or as a partner, shareholder or officer of an organisation that has a relationship with the company). For example, should a family member of a director be an *officer* of the company, the director cannot be deemed independent.

Ownership of stock or affiliation with a dominant shareholder, does not itself preclude a board of directors from determining that an individual is independent. However, if the qualified shareholdings is of at least 10%, CMVM's Regulation 7/2001, as amended, determines that such board member cannot be independent.

Furthermore, the board is also free to question the independence of its members, in the light of the emergence of new information.

8.1.2. The Annual Report on Corporate Governance Compliance

According to regulation 7/2001, as amended by regulation 11/2003, companies must prepare an annual report on corporate governance compliance.

Effectively the "comply or disclose" clause, previously included in paragraph 2 of the annex to regulation 7/2001 as amended, has now been shifted, unchanged, to a new chapter, according to which wherever the company fails to comply with any of the CMVM recommendations, it must provide justification for this non-compliance.

The annex to Regulation 7/2001 as amended, has introduced a new chapter 0, which regulates the duty of disclosure of every recommendation followed by the company as well as those recommendations that were not applied in full, along with the justifications for that lack of compliance.

Chapter I of the annex stipulates the information that the report must contain:
1- Diagrams showing the distribution of responsibilities between departments of the company;
2- Description of developments as regards the quotation of shares in the issuing company;
3- Description of the company's policy for the assessment of dividends; the new version of the annex adds the need to disclose the value of every share distributed over the last three financial years;
4- Detailed description of the schemes for the allotment of buy options for shares adopted or valid in the financial year in question and disclosure (and justification) of any share inalienability clauses;

5- Reference to the existence of an Investor Relations desk or any similar, and description of a number of details concerning it, namely the company's website on the Internet;

6- List and description of the committees created by the company, namely an ethics committee or a committee for the assessment of corporate structure and governance;

7- Description of transactions made between the company and members of its board(s), committees and departments, or any relevant owners of preference shares, or held and parent companies;

8- Disclosure of the independent and the non-independent members of the remuneration committee.

9- Disclosure of auditors' remuneration and of auditing services fees.

Chapter II of the annex to Regulation 7/2001 as amended, stipulates which information must be disclosed in the report regarding the exercise of voting and representation rights by shareholders. Paragraphs 1, 2, 3, 5 and 6 of chapter II correspond to the information already required by regulation 7/2001, in relation to statutory rules on the exercise of voting rights, namely concerning postal voting, the introduction of the possibility of electronic voting, existence of a mandatory time period between the receipt of votes and the general meeting and determination of the number of shares required to exercise voting rights. However, paragraph 4 adds the requirement to supply information concerning the required time period in advance for the depositing or blocking of shares that will give the right to participate in and vote at general meetings.

Chapter III of the annex to Regulation 7/2001, as amended, stipulates the information, which must be disclosed by the report:

- Description of internal procedures adopted to monitor risks inherent to the activities of the company

- Indication of existing caps on voting rights, of special rights held by any shareholder, or shareholder agreements that the company is aware of.

- Codes of conduct adopted by the company regarding all matters in general, as for instance, codes of conduct in conflicts of interest, secrecy and incompatibility, and the means provided to the shareholders for accessing those codes and regulations

Chapter IV of the annex to regulation 7/2001, as amended, concerning the management structure, stipulates which information must be disclosed by the report:

- Nature of the management and identification of the board members, with differentiation of board members who are executive and those who are non executive, as well as, those who are independent and those who are not independent as well as positions held by board members in other companies of the same group;

- Existence of an executive committee, or other committees, with management duties; including a description of the duties and composition of those committees, as well as, discrimination of independent and non-independent members;

- Indication of whether the remuneration of the members of the management body is dependent on the results of the company or share price performance;

- Indication of payments awarded to all members of the board, distinguishing between executive and non-executive members and the fixed and the variable part of the remuneration, disclosing the amounts paid by other companies of the same group;

- Description of how the board exercises effective control over the company, particularly information regarding:

> a) matters brought before the executive committee;
>
> b) matters that are not open for discussion in the executive committee;
>
> c) number of meetings held by the management body during the year in question;
>
> d) procedures put in place to ensure that the members of the board are aware of the subject discussed by and decisions made by the executive committee and information disclosed to this effect;
>
> e) distribution of competences between the president of the board and the president of the executive committee;
>
> f) confidentiality duties concerning matters discussed in the board;
>
> g) conflicts of interest within the board, and the maximum number of positions which directors may hold in the boards of other companies.

8.2. Exercise of Shareholder Rights

8.2.1. Exercise of Shareholder Voting and Representation Rights

The CMVM recommendations, begin by motivating companies to encourage shareholders to make an active use of their voting rights and to counter the absence of shareholders in general meetings, through, for example, postal voting. As per the amendments to the

Recommendations, the active use of voting rights, whether directly or by proxy, should never be limited by statutory restrictions (Recommendation II/2).

Voting by proxy, by one shareholder or more than five shareholders, is governed by article 380 and 381 of the Portuguese Companies Code, which ensure that the shareholder is provided with clear and complete information on the matters to be discussed and voted on a general meeting. These principles are developed by article 23 of the Portuguese Securities Code.

8.2.2. Exercise of Minority Shareholders' Rights

Given that the share ownership is concentrated in the hands of a limited number of shareholders (as in much of Europe), the interests of the minority shareholders require significant protection, as their influence is week in comparison to that of the bigger shareholders.

Protecting these minority shareholders' rights is an issue of utmost importance in Portuguese Company Law and is effected through the Portuguese Companies Code and Portuguese Securities Code.

Pursuant to its provisions, minority shareholders have, in certain circumstances, rights on the appointment and removal of Directors, veto powers over certain management and policy matters, powers to call a general meeting and to file proceedings against directors who have failed to protect the rights of the company, access to information, rights to influence the dividend distribution policy, rights concerning the dilution of equity stakes and transfer of shares, and also the power to block a transfer of nominative shares.

The Portuguese Securities Code also provides protection to minority shareholders, who, after the launch of a takeover bid, are left directly or indirectly, with less than 10% of the voting rights attributable to the share capital of the target company. Their stake must then be acquired within six months of the closing of the offer (compulsory takeover bid or "squeezing out mechanism"). Should the abovementioned shareholder fail to forward a proposal to buy out minority shareholdings, each of the minority shareholders can force, in writing, the acquirer to make an offer for the shares ("compulsory sale mechanism"), which is effective from the date of notification of CMVM to the controlling shareholder. Moreover, in compulsory acquisition proceedings, equal treatment to holders of shares of the same class must be assured, in particular with regard to the calculation of the consideration of the shares.

8.3. Defensive Devices Against Takeover Bids

Defensive devices prevent proper functioning of the stock market. A balanced separation of interests between shareholders and directors may be the answer so that the so-called market for corporate control ensures reliable corporate management.

Some of the most important consequences of these defensive devices are that remote and outside shareholders, not having management control nor being able to exercise the voting rights corresponding to their shareholdings, see their shares highly depreciated.

- CMVM differentiates between "benign" defensive devices and those incompatible with the shareholders' interests;
- Defensive devices against takeover bids are incompatible with the shareholders' interests wherever they seek to frustrate hostile takeover bids at all costs, thereby protecting the interests of the incumbent managers rather than the interests of the shareholders, as hostile takeover bids are often considered the most effective tools shareholders have to replace badly performing managers;
- Amongst such devices are those designed to decrease automatically the value of the company's assets in case of a takeover bid (the so-called *poison pills*), two of which are expressly outlawed by the Portuguese Securities Code:

    a) Issuance of new shares from the moment the target company has knowledge of the takeover bid (i.e., from the date of disclosure of the preliminary announcement) to the final assessment of the result - often acquired by a friendly third party, the so-called *white knight*;

    b) Disposal of important parts of the company's assets (or *crown jewels*), from the date of disclosure of the preliminary announcement to the final assessment of the result;

Another well-known example of a protectionist device against hostile takeovers is the limitation, set out in the Articles of Association, of the maximum voting rights held by each shareholder, irrespective of the actual size of its participation in the company's share capital (voting caps, known in Portuguese as *"blindagem de estatutos"* (literally, "armouring the company's Articles of Association)).

These kinds of defensive devices leave Portuguese listed companies with reduced trade in the stock exchange and therefore with low market capitalisation. In fact, the majority of the first twenty listed companies in the Portuguese market can hardly be, in practice, the object of a takeover bid. The levels of free-float in most of the companies listed in the Portuguese Stock Index ("PSI") 20 are under 50% and the four listed companies that have more than half of their capital in free-float are only theoretically open to takeover bids.

8.4. Board of Directors

According to article 278 of the Portuguese Companies Code, the management structure may consist of a unitary structure of management or of a two-tier structure. The first one - which is the most popular in Portugal - is composed of a board of directors overseen by an board of auditors, and the second one is composed of single manager or a board of a maximum of 5 members and an advisory board, which are overseen by a single external qualified auditor. Recommendation IV/5, states that the board of directors should be composed of a mixture of members who ensure effective management, assembling no less than twice a month.

Article 407/3 4 and 5 of the Portuguese Companies Code states that the board of directors - the unitary structure of management - may create an executive committee for daily management. Its powers may not include those decisions, which can affect company control or assets and thus company or shareholders interests.

The relationship between the executive committee and board of directors must be governed by carefully drafted internal procedures, in accordance with the principle of transparency, and the board must be permanently and regularly informed of the committee's activities.

The recommendations advise companies to create internal control committees for the assessment of matters from which actual or potential conflicts of interests may arise, such as the nomination of directors and managers, remuneration policy, assessment of corporate structure and governance.

8.4. 1. Remuneration Policy

A set of procedures concerning the compensation schemes and policies should be outlined and implemented by a remuneration committee drawn from the board. In addition, directors' fees, especially those connected with daily management, should be based on independent market surveys and should be connected to profits.

According to CMVM´s Regulation 7/2001, as amended, listed companies must report on plans for the allotment of shares and/or stock options among employees and/or members of the board of directors. This information, must include the justification for the adoption of the policy, conditions attached to the allotment, criteria concerning the price of shares and stock options, the validity of such options, the number of shares to be issued and characteristics of the same, the existence of incentives to purchase shares and/or stock options and the competence of the board of directors to carry out or amend the plan.

Article 399/1 Portuguese Companies Code stipulates that remuneration of the directors is determined by the general meeting or by a committee designated by the general meeting and Recommendation IV/10 states that the members of this remunerations committee should be independent. The concept of independence can be found above.

8.5. Institutional Investors

Those entities, which can be considered institutional investors, are listed in article 30 of the Portuguese Securities Code, as follows:

i) Credit institutions;

ii) Investment companies;

iii) Collective investment institutions and their holding companies;

iv) Insurance companies; and

v) Pension funds holding companies.

According to the CMVM Recommendations, institutional investors should make an active and diligent use of their voting and information rights and disclose information on their policies towards the companies in whom they invest.

The final outcome of the amendments to the CMVM Recommendations does not consist of altering their general sense and that of the CMVM Regulations, but of advising specific measures for improving corporate governance and adapting them to the changes already being encouraged at an international level.

In fact, all the most recent reforms in the legal and regulatory framework regarding corporate governance (such as the European Commission's Action Plan), are united by a common purpose: to encourage listed companies to achieve a higher management and performance standards, characterised by clearness and transparency, which will prevent the occurrence of other "corporate scandals", such as, the most recent examples such as Enron's or, more recently, Parmalat's.

Institutional investors play an important role in corporate governance matters as their independent and critical analysis provides an invaluable assessment of the performance of the companies they invest in. Such scrutiny may also stimulate improvement in the company's management performance.

CMVM is, therefore, at this stage, actively promoting good corporate governance practices, so that disclosure, transparency and equality of rights between shareholders become paramount for Portuguese companies. It seems that CMVM is determined to ensure that companies perform well and protect all investors. The achievement of these objectives will be obtained through "…monitoring, rewarding and sanctioning managers, generally making them accountable…"[1], through continuous review of the corporate governance regulatory framework in step with the developments in the country's economy.

---

[1] Borges, António, Corporate Governance… …*Lisbon stirs the debate,*
http://www.ebfonline.com/at_forum/at_forum.asp?id=348&linked=345

EMPLOYMENT LAW
CHAPTER 9

The Main Features of Employment Agreements

9.1. International Treaties

Portuguese employment law originates in a number of international treaties to which Portugal is a signatory or has acceded to such as:

- The 1948 Universal Declaration of Human Rights (UDHR), which enshrines, *inter alia*, the freedom of choice of employment, the principle of equal treatment, the protection of the unemployed;

- The International Labour Organisation (ILO), whose recommendations and conventions have been adopted by Portugal (it has ratified more than 70 ILO conventions);

- The 1950 European Convention for the Protection of Human Rights and Fundamental Freedoms (European Convention on Human Rights);

- The 1961 European Social Charter (whose 1996 revised version was formally ratified by Portugal in 2001), adopted by the Member States of the Council of Europe.

- The 2000 Charter of Fundamental Rights of the European Union, proclaiming the common values of human dignity, freedom, equality and solidarity.

9.2. European Union Policy

Pursuant to the principles enshrined in the European Social Charter, in 1989, 11 of the then 12 EEC Member States adopted several guidelines on employment and social policy, contained in the document known as the Community Charter of the Fundamental Social Rights of Workers (Social Charter), which stated that the completion of the internal market should lead to an improvement in living and working conditions in the EU. This would be achieved through the harmonisation of such conditions in the Member States, particularly the duration and organisation of working time and forms of employment other than open-ended agreements, such as fixed term, part-time, temporary or seasonal employment agreements.

The Social Charter was further complemented by an agreement on social policy signed in 1991 by the same 11 Member States, annexed to the Social Protocol incorporated in the Maastricht

Treaty. The agreement allowed the 11 signatories to pursue the Social Protocol's more ambitious objectives rather than just abide by the Maastricht Treaty's provisions on social policy. However, in 1997, the UK - the Member State which had refused to participate initially - adopted the Social Protocol. As a result, the agreement's provisions were incorporated in, and the Social Protocol abrogated by, the 1997 Amsterdam Treaty, which thus featured enlarged and deepened provisions on social and employment policy.

Several Directives were enacted in order to achieve European Social and employment policy flowing from the Social Charter and the Amsterdam Treaty.

Finally, in 2000, the Charter of Fundamental Rights of the European Union was approved, containing a specific provision concerning "the freedom to choose an occupation and the right to engage in work" for citizens of the European Union and nationals of third countries in the territory of Member States.

9.3. Constitutional Background

Pursuant to the principles laid down in the UDHR, the 1976 Constitution of the Portuguese Republic (last revised in 2001), enshrines several fundamental rights and freedoms with regard to employment: the freedom of choice of employment; the principle of stability and continuity of the employment relationship, namely the prohibition of termination of the employment agreement without just cause or on political or ideological grounds; the right to employment; the fundamental rights of employees, such as the right to receive a fair and equitable salary, to have a rest period and to periodic leave with pay and to safety and health protection.

9.4. Legal Framework for Employment Agreements

9.4.1. Portuguese Legal Framework

Employment agreements are governed by Law 99/2003 of 27th August since December 2003, which condenses most of the Portuguese legal framework on employment law in one sole piece of legislation. This legal guide aims to characterize the fundamental guidelines of this framework as per its most recent amendments.

The new provisions indicate the hierarchy of sources of labour law in relation to employment agreements, as follows:

i)   Employment legislation;

ii)   Collective labour agreements;

iii)   The terms of the employment agreement;

iv)   Company and/or professional practices and customs (unless they violate the law or are disregarded by the parties).

9.4.2. Criteria to determine the Law Applicable to Employment Agreements

Portuguese courts have consistently held that, where an employment agreement overlaps the legal systems of more than one country (i.e., the employee is a Portuguese citizen working outside Portugal for a Portuguese-resident employer), the law in force in the location of the workplace shall apply (*lex loci laboris*), unless otherwise agreed by the parties.

Law 99/2003, however, now states that the law chosen by the parties governs the contract, and that only in the absence of contractual stipulation, will the law most closely connected to the agreement apply. This connection is usually related to the location of the workplace.

9.5 The Main Features of Employment Agreements

9.5.1 Form of Agreement

In certain cases, an employment agreement is only valid if laid down in writing. This requirement applies to the following situations:

i)   promissory employment agreements;

ii) fixed-term employment agreements;

iii) temporary work agreements.

9.5.2. Duration

Employment agreements can be concluded either for an undetermined period of time or for a fixed term.

Since fixed term employment agreements are deemed by the legislator to be an exception to the principle of stability and continuity of the employment relationship enshrined in the Constitution, they can only be concluded under certain circumstances strictly stipulated in the law, such as:

    (i)   Substitution of an employee on leave for the duration of the same;

    (ii) Seasonal or sporadic activities;

    (iii) A temporary and/or unexpected increase in the company's activities;

    (iv) Direction, execution or oversight of public works projects or of projects outside the company's normal activities;

    (v) A new activity, with an uncertain duration;

    (vi) Recruitment of employees searching for a first job or unemployed for a long time.

Such circumstances as well as the length of the term must be expressly stated in detail in the employment agreement, which must also contain full information as regards the identity of the parties, the employee's functions and remuneration, working conditions, and the date of conclusion and/or of commencement of the agreement. Failure to comply with these requirements results in the nullification of the fixed term clause and in the conversion of the fixed term employment agreement into one for an undetermined period.

A fixed term employment agreement can be renewed three times, up to a maximum of six years in total (initial term plus renewals). In the case of employees searching for a first job, the total limit on the duration of the contract is reduced to two years (including renewals).

If it exceeds these limits, it is automatically converted into an employment agreement for an undetermined period.

9.5.3. Working Hours

As a rule, working hours are a maximum 8 hours per day and 40 hours per week. Working hours and overtime remuneration rules can be modified, to the benefit of the employee, by collective labour agreements. Overtime should be remunerated in addition to the normal remuneration per working hour, at the following rates:

    i) For the first hour - 50%

    ii) For every additional hour - 75%

    iii) During the weekly rest period and official holidays - 100%

The employer is only responsible for paying overtime-working hours where he has previously and expressly determined the necessity of overtime work.

As a rule, employees are entitled to a mandatory rest period of one day plus a second complementary day, which usually occur on Saturdays and Sundays for each seven-day period.

Daily and weekly working hours are scheduled by the employer and must be complied with by employees, who can only be exempted of such an obligation in certain cases, such as that of employees in executive positions.

9.5.4. Leave with Pay

Employees are entitled to an annual 22-working day period of leave with pay (i.e., to take leave and receive their regular salary plus an allowance equal to that salary), except if working under a fixed-term employment agreement of less than six months in length. In this case employees are only entitled to a two-day leave with pay, per month.

9.5.5. Protection of Motherhood and Fatherhood

Employment legislation in Portugal provides for an ample protection of pregnant female employees as well as those who have given birth recently and of male employees who have recently fathered a child, *inter alia*:

(i) Female employees who are pregnant or have recently given birth, are entitled to take leave from work for pre -or post- natal medical exams and for breast-feeding purposes, as well as being entitled to a 120-day maternity leave;

(ii) Male employees who have recently fathered a child are entitled to a 5-day leave within the first month after the child's birth, which can be extended to a period equal to the abovementiond maternity leave under certain circumstances (death or physical or psychical disablement of the child's mother, or the joint decision of both parents);

(iii) Parents of children less than 10 years old are entitled to 30-day parental leaves for assisting their children in case of illness or accident.

9.5.6. Termination of the Employment Agreement

An employment agreement can only be terminated according to the following terms and conditions:

i) Retirement or supervening permanent disablement of the employee;

ii) Cancellation of the agreement under mutual consent, which must be given in a written document signed by both parties;

iii) Termination of the contract by the employee on his own initiative, with prior notification to the employer either delivered at least 30 days in advance (60 days if the agreement has been in force for more than two years) or effective immediately where the agreement is terminated on grounds of just cause (e.g., breach of contract by the employer);

iv) Non-renewal of a fixed term agreement by the employer or by the employee, if notified to the other party in writing at least, respectively, fifteen or eight days in advance of the date of expiration of the term (renewal is automatic in the absence of such notification);

v) Collective dismissal of a group of employees (at least two or five, wherever the company has two to fifty or more than fifty employees, respectively), on grounds of staff reduction or partial or total shutdown of the company for economic, technological or structural reasons, which requires prior notification both to the targeted employees and the trade union representatives within the company, negotiation of the terms of the dismissal with the latter, assisted by government representatives for labour affairs (who ensure that the negotiation procedures are regular and arbitrate disputes between the company and trade union representatives) and compensation of the targeted employees;

vi) Dismissal of an individual employee on the grounds of the redundancy of his post for economic, technological or structural reasons (i.e., decrease in the company's activity, company restructuring or partial or total shutdown of the company), which entails prior notification both to the targeted employee and to trade union representatives within the company (either of them can oppose the dismissal through a reasoned opinion in writing addressed to the company) prior to a final decision as well as mandatory compensation of the targeted employee;

vii) Dismissal on grounds of the employee's maladjustment to his post following technological modifications thereof, which can only take place if such maladjustment is verified despite (a) vocational training by the employee, (b) an adjustment period and (c) the offer to the employee of a compatible post;

viii) Dismissal on grounds of just cause:

a) Just cause is verified where the employee's behaviour gravely hinders or renders impossible the continuation of the employment relationship, as per the formulation of Decree-Law 99/2003;

b) The dismissal can only take place upon completion of disciplinary out-of-court proceedings (usually carried out by the employer's personnel manager or by a legal counsel or lawyer) whereby the grounds of just cause for dismissal are conclusively verified;

c) The decision to dismiss the employee can be challenged by him before the Labour Courts, where he can plead for the precautionary suspension of the same, where appropriate, and for its annulment. Where the dismissal decision is effectively annulled by the Labour Courts, the employee is entitled to opt for reinstatement with payment of all the salaries owed since the date of the unfair dismissal, or compensation.

The courts may decide, at the employer's request, not to reinstate unfairly dismissed employees, if their return could cause serious disruption to the company's business, in the case of small companies, or if the employee occupies a management post.

9.6. Temporary Employment Agreements

As temporary employment agreements are also considered by the legislator as an exception to the principle of stability and continuity of the employment relationship, such agreements, as well as access to, and carrying out of, temporary employment activities, are subject to the fairly detailed provisions of Decree-Law 358/89, of 17th October 1989, amended by Law 39/96 of 31st August 1996 and Law 146/99 of 1st September 1999.

A temporary employment relationship entails the conclusion of two separate agreements:

a) A Temporary Employment Agreement concluded in writing between a temporary employment company and an employee, whereby the latter undertakes to work for, and under the control of, a third party making use of his services (user), on a temporary basis, in return for remuneration paid by the temporary employment company, which must also pay the employee's Social Security contributions as well as a mandatory insurance policy in favour of the employee and retains disciplinary powers over the employee;

b) An utilisation agreement, concluded in writing between a temporary employment company and a third party (user), whereby the former assigns, on a temporary basis, an employee to work for and under the control of the user, in return for a certain consideration (usually determined on an hourly basis). The assigned employee's tasks, workplace and working hours, as well as his leave with pay, if taken during the assignment, are scheduled by the user, which thus acts as the employee's *de facto* employer.

As the credibility of the temporary employment relationship depends on the credibility of the temporary employment company itself, only companies licensed by the government are allowed to carry out temporary employment activities. Such licenses are awarded only if the company meets fairly tight criteria on its moral, legal and financial ability to carry out temporary employment activities.

The sole exception is the sporadic assignment of employees between companies, foreseen in the new employment legislation, which is only possible where allowed by a collective agreement, or in absence thereof, where *(i)* the assigned employee is hired by the assignor under an undetermined period of employment agreement, *(ii)* the assigned employee expressly agrees to the assignment, *(iii)* the assignor and assignee are legally or economically dependent on each other, *(iv)* the duration of the assignment may not be of more than one year.

9.7. Statutory Regime of Foreign Workers in Portugal

Portuguese rules set out certain specific provisions on the employment of foreigners within Portugal. Thus, foreigners legally allowed to stay or reside in the country, and to work therein under an employment agreement, have the same rights and obligations as Portuguese employees.

The employment agreement must be concluded in writing and comply with the formalities required by the specific legislation. These requirements do not apply to employees from countries that are members of the European Economic Area or that practise/implement the equality of rights between national and foreign workers.

According to Decree-Law 99/2003, the provisions applicable to foreign workers also apply to stateless persons.

9.8. Social Security Contributions

Persons hired under an employment agreement are required to enrol in and pay a contribution to the Social Security fund. This contribution is actually supported in part by the employer and in part by the employee. The amount of such contributions as well as the employer and employee's respective shares therein are set out in Law 17/2000 of 8th August 2000 (Social Security Framework Law) and laid out in other Chapter of this Guide.

INSURANCE

CHAPTER 10

10.1. Introduction

European Union policy was designed to make it easier for insurance companies with a head office in an EU Member State to cover risks arising within other EU Member States through the introduction of the right to establishment and provide services in the internal market for insurance.

10.2. European Union Legal Framework

The internal market for insurance builds chiefly on:

- Council Directives 73/239/EEC of 24th July 1973 (First non-Life Insurance Directive), as amended by European Parliament and of the Council Directive 2000/26/CE of 16th May 2000, and 79/267/EEC of 5th March 1979 (First Life Insurance Directive), which provided for the effective exercise of the freedom of establishment and ;

- Council Directives 88/357/EEC of 22nd June 1988 (Second non-Life Insurance Directive), as amended by European Parliament and of the Council Directive 2000/26/CE of 16th May 2000, and 90/232/EEC of 14th May 1990 (Second Life Assurance Directive, which provided for the effective exercise of the freedom to provide services; and

- Council Directives 92/49/EEC of 18th June 1992 (Third non-Life Insurance Directive) and Directive 92/96/EEC of 10th November 1992 (Third Life Assurance Directive), both amended by European Parliament and of the Council Directive 2002/87/EC of 12th November, which amended the previous directives and created a single authorisation or "passport" for insurance companies;

- Directive 2002/83/EC of the European Parliament and of the Council of 5th November 2002 concerning life assurance.

Indeed, the Third Life Assurance and non-Life Insurance Directives harmonised insurance legislation to achieve mutual recognition of authorisations and control systems, thereby making it possible to grant authorisation, via a single licence valid throughout the Community and apply the principle of supervision by the home Member State.

Therefore, an insurance company can carry out its activities throughout the Community, either by exercising the right of establishment or the freedom to provide services, under a single official licence granted by the competent authorities of the Member State in which it has its head office, without having to seek a new licence in the host Member State.

These directives also gave the insurance supervisory authorities of the Member States the necessary supervision powers to ensure that insurance companies carry out their activities in a regular manner throughout the Community, whether under the right of establishment or the freedom to provide services, in particular, the power to introduce appropriate safeguards or impose sanctions aimed at preventing irregularities and infringements of the provisions on insurance supervision.

The Third Life and Non-Life Insurance Directives were implemented in Portugal by Decree-Law 102/94, of 20th April 1994, revoked by Decree-Law 94-B/98, of 17th April 1998.

10.3. Portuguese Legal Framework

Insurance and reinsurance in Portugal is governed, in essence, by the following legislation:

(i) Decree-Law 94-B/98 of 17th April 1998, as amended by Decrees-Law 8-C/2002 of 11th January 2002, 169/2002 of 25th July, 72-A/2003 de 14th April and 90/2003 of 30th April, which regulates the access to, and carrying out of, insurance and reinsurance activities within the European Community by insurance companies with their head offices in Portugal, as well as the provision of insurance and reinsurance services in Portugal by insurance companies with their head offices abroad;

(ii) Articles 96 to 102, 425 to 462 and 595 to 615 of the 1888 Commercial Code, containing common provisions on insurance contracts;

(iii) Decree-Law 176/95, of 26th July 1995, adding provisions on the legal framework for insurance contracts and transparency duties of insurance companies;

(iv) Decree-Law 289/2001 of 13th November 2001, introducing the legal framework for the national insurance supervisory authority, the *Instituto de Seguros de Portugal* (Portuguese Insurance Institute).

10.4. Access to and Exercise of Insurance and Reinsurance Activities

10.4.1. Common Requirements

Any company which desires to accede to, and provide, insurance and/or reinsurance services must comply with the requirements imposed by Decree-Law 94-B/98. explained in the following sections.

10.4.1.1. Entities which may carry out the Business of Insurance

Insurance services can only be provided by authorised corporations with their head offices in Portugal, authorised mutual associations, branches of insurance companies with their head offices in other European Union Member States that meet all applicable requirements, authorised branches of insurance companies with their head offices outside European Union territory, authorised state-owned insurance companies or European companies authorised in accordance with the applicable legislation.

10.4.1.2. Prior Authorisation

The abovementioned entities - except branches of insurance companies, or of European companies, with their head offices in other EU Member States - can only carry out their activities under a prior licence granted by the Instituto de Seguros de Portugal (*Instituto de Seguros de Portugal*) or, in certain cases, by the Minister of Finance.

The licence is valid for the whole European Union territory if granted to insurance companies with their head office in Portugal and for Portuguese territory only if granted to branches of insurance companies with their head offices outside the European Union.

10.4.1.3. Prudential Guarantees

Insurance companies must provide the following prudential guarantees:

(i) Requirements adequate to enable the company to fulfil the obligations flowing from insurance contracts;

(ii) An adequate solvency margin, equal to the value of the sum of the business's assets, minus the value of foreseeable liabilities and the value of the intangible assets;

(iii) A guarantee fund equal to a third of the value of the solvency margin but not lower than certain minimum limits.

10.4.1.4. Reinsurance

Reinsurance activities can be carried out by insurance companies incorporated under Portuguese law or by foreign entities, whether established or represented in Portugal or not, which are authorised to provide reinsurance activities in their home country.

10.4.2. Access to and Provision of Insurance Services by Companies with Head offices in Portugal

10.4.2.1. Common Requirements

(i) An insurance company with its head office in Portugal must be incorporated as a corporation and bear a corporate name which clearly indicates that its object is to carry out insurance activities.

(ii) It must have a share capital of at least 7,500,000 euros whenever the company deals either with non-life insurance (2,500,000 euros if it deals only with health or legal expenses or care insurance) or with life assurance only, or of at least 15,000,000 euros if its deals with both non-life insurance and life assurance;

(iii) The incorporation can only take place under a prior licence granted by the *Instituto de Seguros de Portugal*.

10.4.2.2. Establishment of Branches in Other European Union Member States

An insurance company with its head office in Portugal, which proposes to open a branch in another European Union Member State, must notify the *Instituto de Seguros de Portugal* of such a proposal.

The *Instituto de Seguros de Portugal* will then notify the competent authorities of the Member State in which the branch is to be opened. Such notification will not however be carried out if the Supervisory Authority has reasons to doubt whether the insurance company's structural organisation or financial situation is adequate to the proposed business or has justified doubts on the reputation or professional qualification of the authorised agent of the branch in question.

The branch may only commence its activities on receiving notification from the competent authority of the Member State where it is located.

10.4.2.3. Provision of Services in Another European Union Member State

An insurance company with its head office in Portugal, proposing to provide services in another European Union Member State must notify the *Instituto de Seguros de Portugal* of such an intention, specifying the nature of the risks or commitments it proposes to cover.

The *Instituto de Seguros de Portugal* must then notify the competent authorities of the Member State where the services will be provided, and also inform the insurance company thereof. The said notification must certify that the insurance company has met the minimum solvency margin required in Portugal and specify which services the company is authorised to provide in Portugal as well as those the company proposes to provide in the aforementioned Member State.

The insurance company may commence the provision of services in question on receiving the abovementioned information.

10.4.3. Establishment of Branches of Insurance Companies with Head Offices in Other European Union Member States

An insurance company with a head office in another EU Member State, proposing to establish a branch in Portugal must comply with the following requirements:

(i) It must notify the competent authorities of the home Member State;

(ii) The abovementioned authorities must then inform the *Instituto de Seguros de Portugal* of the insurance company's intention to exercise the right of establishment in Portugal;

(iii) The *Instituto de Seguros de Portugal* must, within two months of receiving the information referred to above, inform the competent authority of the home Member State, if appropriate, of the conditions under which, in the interest of the general good, that activity must be carried out in Portugal;

(iv) On receiving a communication from the *Instituto de Seguros de Portugal* or, if no communication is received from it, on expiry of the abovementioned period, the branch may be established and start operating;

(v) To provide insurance services, that branch must comply with the requirements and conditions applying in respect thereof to insurance companies with their head offices in Portugal.

10.4.4. Establishment of Branches of Insurance Companies with Head Office Outside the European Union

An insurance company with a head office outside the European Union, proposing to establish a branch in Portugal must comply with the requirements described below.

10.4.4.1. Specific and Prior Authorisation

A non-EU insurance company requires prior authorisation to provide insurance services in Portugal. Such authorisation is granted:

(i) By the Minister of Finance with the consent of the *Instituto de Seguros de Portugal* or by the latter, under delegation of powers, on a case-by-case basis;

(ii) To insurance companies that have been incorporated for more than five years alone;

(iii) To provide life assurance services alone, if the insurance company provides both life insurance and non-life assurance services in its home country;

(iv) To provide insurance services in Portugal within the same classes of insurance as those covered by the authorisation granted to the insurance company by the competent authorities of its home country.

10.4.4.2. Requirements for the Application of Authorisation

An insurance company with its head office outside the EU, must provide the following information, on applying for authorisation to establish a branch in Portugal:

a) A statement of the reasons justifying the establishment of the branch in Portugal;

b) An explanatory memorandum of its international activities and, in particular, of their relationship with the Portuguese insurance market;

c) A copy of its Memorandum and Articles of Association;

d) A list of its directors, containing their respective identification;

e) Balance sheets, trading accounts, and profit and loss accounts for the last three financial years;

f) A certificate, issued by the competent authorities of the applicant's home country no less than 90 days prior to the date of application, attesting that the insurance company was duly incorporated and exists under the laws in force in its home country and specifying which types and/or classes of insurance are covered by the authorisation granted to the same company.

10.4.4.3. Specific Advantages with regard to Prudential Guarantees

The branch of an insurance company with a head office in a non-European Union country is required to observe the following with regard to prudential guarantees:

(i) It must meet its financial requirements by means of a deposit at the *Instituto de Seguros de Portugal*.

(ii) It must have a solvency margin adequate to the totality of its activities in Portugal.

(iii) The assets representing the solvency margin must be located in Portugal up to the amount of the guarantee fund and the excess within the European Union.

However, the same insurance company may apply to the Minister of Finance, through the ISP, for the following exceptions, by way of derogation from the abovementioned requirements:

(i) The deposit required for securing the technical provisions may be dispensed with, on condition that the company proves that it has made a deposit in another EU Member State, equal a half of the guarantee fund it is required to provide in relation to the entire business which it undertakes in Portugal and in the other EU Member States;

(ii) The solvency margin is calculated in relation to all the business carried out by the company in Portugal and in the other EU Member States;

(iii) The assets representing the guarantee fund may be located in any other EU Member State.

The advantages set out above may only be granted if they were also applied for with, and agreed by, the competent authorities of all Member States from which the company has requested or obtained authorisation.

The state of solvency of the entire business of the branches within the Community shall be supervised in the future by the competent authority of one of the Member States, chosen by the company in question. Such supervision is to be exercised by the *Instituto de Seguros de Portugal* should it be chosen as the supervision authority.

These exceptional dispensations may be withdrawn at the request of one or more Member States, provided that the withdrawal is made simultaneously in all the Member States in which the applicant operates.

10.4.5. Provision of Services in Portugal by Insurance Companies with Head Office in Another European Union Member State

Under the freedom to provide services, an insurance company with its head office in another EU Member State may cover risks or commitments located within Portugal through its head office.

The same company is required to join and participate in the schemes designed to guarantee the payment of compensation to insured persons and injured third parties, relating to liability for accidents at work or to liability in respect of the use of motor vehicles (except the liability of the carrier) as well as to pay the legally required contributions to the *Fundo de Garantia Automóvel* (Motor Vehicle Guarantee Fund) and to the *Fundo de Acidentes de Trabalho* (Workers' Compensation Fund), under the terms and conditions applicable to insurance companies with their head office in Portugal.

Furthermore, if the said company intends to cover risks subject to compulsory insurance in Portugal, it must inform the *Instituto de Seguros de Portugal* of the name and address of a Portuguese-resident representative who will possess all the necessary information and will be duly empowered to act as a representative of the company, before injured parties, the Portuguese judicial and administrative authorities, including the *Instituto de Seguros de Portugal*, with regard to claims for compensation covered by such insurance, as well as to proceed with the payment thereof. The representative is not allowed to provide any direct insurance service on behalf of the company represented.

10.5. Transparency and Insurance Contracts

Insurance contracts are governed by the 1888 Commercial Code, which contains common provisions on the form, contents and premium of the insurance contract.

Decree-Law 176/95 of 26th July 1995 added the legal framework governing insurance contracts, in order to cope with the change in insurance contract law imposed by the creation of the single market in the insurance sector, which opened a new area to competition, resulting in a larger and more complex supply of products (particularly in the field of personal insurance) and in a wider range of coverage, exclusions and other conditions. The above mentioned Decree-Law lays out transparency duties in contract relations, namely information duties to be satisfied before and during the execution of the contract, including a vast set of minimum requirements regarding the contents of the contract. Such information duties are further complemented - chiefly with regard to life assurance - by certain provisions of Decree-Law 94-B/98.

10.6. Pension Funds

The authorisation, establishment and management of pension funds, as well as the incorporation and pursuit of the business of pension fund management companies, are governed by Decree-Law 475/99 of 9th November 1999, as amended by Decree-Law 292/2001 of 20th November 2001.

Decree-Law 475/99 provides protection devices for contributors, members, beneficiaries as well as sponsors, namely a set of requirements imposed on pension fund management companies with regard to the form and contents of the contracts concluded with the former and the right to a cooling-off period for individual contributors to open-ended pension funds. The abovementioned Decree-Law also imposes prudential rules with regard to the management of pension funds and to pension fund-managing companies.

10.7. The Portuguese Insurance Supervisory Authority (*"Instituto de Seguros de Portugal"*)

The ever-growing complexity of products related to insurance and pension funds requires increased supervision powers by the competent authorities.

The *Instituto de Seguros de Portugal* is the insurance supervisory authority for Portugal. It is a legal entity governed by public law with administrative and financial autonomy, its main source of revenue being the charges paid by those entities subject to its supervision.

The *Instituto de Seguros de Portugal,* ensures that insurers and pension funds are in a position to meet their commitments, enforces insurance and pension fund law, supervises the relations between consumers and insurers and pension fund management companies.

The *Instituto de Seguros de Portugal* has the following powers:

a)   Regulatory Powers:
- To draft, at the request of the Government or on its own initiative, proposals for legislation governing the business of insurance.

- To design technical regulations and instructions of a binding nature for entities under its supervision.

b) Supervision Powers:

- To authorise the access to and supervise the provision of insurance and reinsurance services, pension fund managing and insurance brokerage by companies with their head offices in Portugal.
- To supervise the activities carried out within the territory of other Member States by companies with their head offices in Portugal.
- To authorise the establishment in non-European Union countries of branches of insurance companies with their head office in Portugal.
- To deliver an opinion on, or authorise under delegation of powers, the establishment in Portugal of a branch of an insurance company with its head office in a non-European country.
- To oversee the compliance by insurers with the applicable legislation and prudential rules, namely by assessing the adequacy of their technical provisions for covering their liabilities as well as that of their solvency margins to cope with the risks of the insurance business.
- To authorise the constitution of pension funds as well as the incorporation of pension fund managing companies and ensure their respective compliance with the law and make regular actuarial audits of the pension funds.
- To oversee the compliance with the law by the policies marketed by the insurance companies by using a non-systematic, sampling method.

c) Management of special funds

The *Instituto de Seguros de Portugal* manages the Special Funds it is entrusted by the law, including:

(i) The *Fundo de Garantia Automóvel* (Motor Vehicle Guarantee Fund) pays compensation to third parties injured in motor vehicle accidents (Decrees-Law 522/85 of 31st December and 72-A/2003 of 14th April):

- In the case of death or physical injury, where the culprit is unknown or has no valid motor vehicle insurance or the insurer has gone into liquidation;
- In the case of damage to property, where the culprit is known but has no valid motor vehicle insurance and the damage is valued at over EUR 299.28.

(ii) The *Fundo de Acidentes de Trabalho* (The Workers' Compensation Fund (WCF) was set up in 1999, by the Decree-Law 142/99 of 30th April 1999, to guarantee:

- The payment of benefits arising from accidents at work whenever the employer is unable to make the payments on account of having gone into receivership or liquidation;

b) The payment of accidents at work insurance premiums at the request of an business unable to do so on account of being in receivership;

c) The updating of accidents at work benefits;

d) The covering of risks insurance companies have refused to cover.

d) Consumer Assistance

The ISP is also empowered to, through its Consumer Assistance Service:

- Inform the public with regard to the services provided by insurance companies, in particular, with regard to the most important contractual clauses, which people and companies should be aware of before signing a contract;

- Inform consumers of their rights under insurance contracts and to advise them how to use those rights more efficiently;

- Deliver an opinion on complaints from the public against insurance companies, brokers and pension funds that are not settled elsewhere.

MADEIRA FREE TRADE ZONE
CHAPTER 11

11.1 - Introduction

The Madeira archipelago, located about 700 km off the Northwest African coast, consists of the islands Madeira and Porto Santo and Desertas, of which Madeira is the largest.

The Portuguese government authorised in 1980 the creation of free trade (i.e., tax-exempt) zones in Madeira and in the Santa Maria island (Azores archipelago) in 1980, in order to stimulate social and economic development in these peripheral regions. In 1986, a framework of specific tax benefits for the Madeira Free Trade Zone (*Zona Franca da Madeira*) was enacted.

Following Portugal's accession to the European Union, the specific Madeira and Santa Maria tax benefits thus created were acknowledged as temporary regional aid schemes for ultra-peripheral regions.

The previous regime authorized by the European Commission expired on 31st December 2000 and was suspended by the Portuguese authorities in 2001 and 2002.

However, the European Commission has authorised a new aid regime for companies setting up in the Industrial Free Trade Zone and the International Services Centre of the Free Trade Zone of Madeira for the period 2003-2006. In its decision, the Commission found that the aid, granted in the form of tax reductions up to the end of 2011, could contribute to the economic diversification of the region. The aid should also compensate for the handicaps brought about by the region's dependence on a small number of sectors (such as tourism and public works).

Access to the International Services Centre is now restricted to the activities included in the list drawn up by the Portuguese authorities on the basis of the statistical classification of economic activities in the European Union (NACE Rev. 1.1.). This list includes services supplied to agriculture, forestry and fisheries, the motor trade including wholesale, transport and communications, real estate, renting and services to business, higher education and adult education, recreational, cultural and sporting activities and personal services.

The new aid regime excludes all financial and insurance intermediary activities, financial and insurance ancillary activities and all "intra-group services" (coordination, accounting and distribution centres).

The purpose of this paper is to outline the current tax benefits applicable to the Madeira Free Trade Zone.

Offshore activities in the Madeira Free Trade Zone ('MTFZ'), also known as the Madeira International Business Centre (MIBC) cover the following four sectors:

a) *International Services* - a broad definition generally encompassing the MTFZ activities of trading, holding, trust managing, consulting, and other service companies,

b) *Financial Services* - the services provided by credit institutions, financial companies and insurance companies or their branches in the MFTZ,

c) *The Industrial Free Trade Zone*- which aims at developing Madeiran industry by attracting manufacturing businesses to the Island of Madeira by granting them specific tax benefits,

d) *The International Shipping Register* (*Registo Internacional de Navios da Madei*ra - MAR), created in 1989 as an alternative to other international registers.

11.2. Basic Legal Framework

Operation in the MFTZ is subject to the following regulations:

The Creation of MIBC
DL 500/80 of 20th October 1980.

Tax and Financial Incentives
DL 165/86, of 26th June 1986.
Art. 33 of DL 215/89, of 1st July 1989, as amended by DL 198/2001, of the 3rd July 2001.

Fees
Order 222/99, of the 28th of December 1999.

Formation, Operation and Registration of Companies

DL 234/88, of the 5th July 1988 (as amended by DL 50/95 of 16th March 1995 and DL 225/95, of 8th September 1995).

DL 212/94, of 10th August 1994.

Financial Activities

DL 10/94, of 13th January 1994.

Industrial Free Trade Zone and International Services

Regulatory Decree 53/82, of 23rd August 1982.

Regional Regulatory Decree 21/87/M, of 5th September 1987 (as amended by Regional Regulatory Decree 23/95/M, of 31st August 1995).

Trust Activity

DL 352-A/88, of the 3rd October 1988 (as amended by DL 264/90, of 31st August 1990).

DL 149/94, of the 25th May 1994.

MAR - International Shipping Register

DL 96/89 of 28th March 1989 (as amended by DL 393/93 of the 23rd November 1993, by DL 5/97 of 9th January 1997, and by DL 331/99 of 20th August 1999)

Order 715/89, of 23rd August 1989.

Order 134/92, of 20th May 1992 (as amended by Order 14/97, of 5th May 1997, by Order 180/99, of 25th October 1999, and by Order 227/99, of 29th December 1999).

Order (R.S.E.E.C.) 135/94, of 1st August 1994 (as amended by Order 227/99 of 29th December 1999).

11.3. New Regime of Companies licensed to carry out Business in the Free Trade Zone of Madeira

The Commission's decision regarding the creation of a new aid scheme for the Free Zone of Madeira for the period 2003-2006 has brought about new tax rates reductions and new restrictions on companies that intend to obtain licences to operate in the Free Trade Zone of Madeira.

Regarding Corporation Tax Rates, all new companies licensed between 1st January 2003 and 31st December 2006 will be able to enjoy a reduced rate of tax of 1% in 2003 and 2004, 2% in 2005 and 2006 and 3% from 2007 until 2011.

To qualify for the privileged tax regime, companies licensed after 1st January 2003, (except pure holding companies "SGPS"), will need to meet specific eligibility criteria, based on the number of new permanent jobs created:

i) Companies that create more than five jobs on the first six months will have access to the regime without further conditions, while those that create between one and five jobs will be eligible only if they make a minimum investment of EUR 75 000 during the first two years of business.

ii) In all cases, the tax benefits will nonetheless be limited by the ceiling placed on the taxable profit which ranges from EUR 1.5 million (where less than three new jobs are created) to EUR 125 million (where more than 100 new jobs are created).

iii) The companies involved will have to start business within a fixed time limit (six months in the case of international services and one year in case of industrial activities), or else the new licenses granted in the free zone will no longer be valid.

11.4. The MFTZ's Areas of Activity
11.4.1. International Services
11.4.1.1. Types of Tax-efficient Vehicles available in the MFTZ

Within the International Services area, operators can make use of a number of corporate vehicles to take advantage of all the tax benefits granted to the MFTZ:

- Pure holding companies
- Mixed holding companies
- Trusts

11.4.1.2. Incorporation/Registration Requirements and Tax Benefits Applicable to such Vehicles

11.4.1.2.1. Pure Holding Companies

(i) Definition - Pure Holding Companies (*Sociedades Gestoras de Participações Sociais - SGPS*) are companies whose corporate object consists solely of managing holdings in other companies. (For definition and scope, please see more detailed information in Chapter 4)

(ii) Tax benefits and exemptions – until 2011, pure holding companies enjoy the following tax benefits:

(a) Full exemption from corporation or individual tax or reduced corporation tax rates, with regard to the dividends and capital gains arising from holdings in non-EU subsidiaries without a permanent establishment in Portugal (except those located in free trade zones). The applicable corporation tax regime depends on the company's licence initial date of operation, as follows:
i) Holding companies licensed before the 31st December 2000, benefit from full exemption from corporation tax.
ii) Holding companies licensed between 1st January 2003 and 31st December 2006, will be able to benefit from a reduced rate of income tax of: 1% in 2003 and 2004, 2% in 2005 and 2006 and 3% from 2007 until 2011.

(b) As regards the dividends paid by EU or Portuguese-resident subsidiaries, they are subject to tax, however, under the Tax Benefit Code pure holding companies are allowed to deduct the totality of such dividends from their taxable income, which in practice is tantamount to a tax exemption on those dividends. Nevertheless the above mentioned deduction must comply with the requirements set out bellow for capital gains.
(c) As regards capital gains and losses realised by " SGPS" arising from holdings in EU or resident companies, on the disposal of shareholdings held for at least one year are not included in the calculation of its taxable profits (i.e. gains exempt and losses not deductible);

(d) In relation to shareholdings acquired from affiliated companies, entities resident in tax heavens or when the company has been transformed into a SGPS, the minimum holding period necessary to exclude the gains from taxation is three years.

(e) No withholding tax applies to dividends paid by resident subsidiaries and those paid by EU subsidiaries may also be exempt from withholding tax, as Madeiran pure holding companies are in a position to qualify as parent companies for the purposes of Council Directive 90/435/EEC of 23rd July 1990 (the Parent/Subsidiary Directive), although that may require a case-by-case study since such qualification is not accepted universally throughout the other EU jurisdictions;

(f) Dividends paid by Madeiran pure holding companies to their non-resident subsidiaries are exempt from individual or corporation tax.

11.4.1.2.2. Mixed Holding Companies

(i) Definition - mixed holding companies are companies whose corporate object consists both of trading in their own right and holding and managing shareholdings in other companies; pursuant to the Portuguese Companies Code, the holding and managing of shareholdings in other companies must be expressly authorised in the company's Articles of Association.

(ii) Legal Forms - A mixed holding company can be incorporated under any of the legal forms provided for in the Portuguese Companies Code, among them: the joint stock company (*sociedade anónima*), the private limited quota company (*sociedade por quotas*) and the sole quotaholder company (*sociedade unipessoal por quotas*);

(iii) Incorporation requirements - a mixed holding company must be incorporated with at least 5 shareholders and a minimum €50,000 share capital, or 2 shareholders and a minimum €5,000 share capital, or 1 shareholder and a minimum €5,000 share capital, if it is incorporated under the form of joint stock company, private limited quota company or sole quotaholder company, respectively. Under Decree-Law 212/94 of 10th August 1994, a joint stock company licensed to operate in Madeira can also be incorporated with a single shareholder;

(iv) Tax benefits and exemptions - mixed holding companies enjoy the following benefits and exemptions until 2011:

(a) Profits arising from operations carried out by mixed holding companies with entities established within the MFTZ or with non-resident entities (whether located within the EU or not) without a permanent establishment in Portugal, are exempt from corporation tax or benefit from a reduced tax rate. The corporation tax regime applicable depends on the date of company's licence to operate in Madeira, as follows;

(b) The interest paid by mixed holding companies operating in the MFTZ in respect of loans made by them is also exempt from corporation tax, provided that such loans were intended for investing within the MFTZ, or supported the company's regular operation, and the grantor is non-resident;

(c) Dividends paid by Madeira mixed holding companies to non-resident shareholders are exempt from corporation or individual income tax, and so is the interest paid by the company in respect of loans or advances granted by non-resident shareholders.

11.4.1.2.3. Trusts

(i) Definition - a trust is a vehicle to which a person or entity (the settlor) allocates certain assets, to be managed by one or more persons (trustees) on behalf of the settlor himself or of a third person (beneficiary) and was introduced in the Portuguese legal system by Decree-Law 352-A/88, of 3rd October 1988 as a means to further stimulate operations in the MFTZ' International Services area;

(ii) Offshore trusts - The aforesaid Decree-Law only allows the incorporation of offshore trusts, those where (a) both the settlor and the beneficiary are non-resident entities (licensed to operate within the MFTZ or not), (b) the immovable assets allocated thereto are located outside Portugal, (c) their income arises from funding from non-resident entities (except bank deposits made with non-resident credit institutions operating within the MFTZ), and (d) the law applicable to the trust is expressly chosen by the settlor;

(iii) Incorporation requirements - the trust must be incorporated through a written document, which must be signed by the settlor or by the trustee on his behalf (whose signature must also be certified by a notary) and contain, *inter alia*, full identification of trust, settlor, trustees and beneficiary, an indication of the type, purpose and assets of the trust, the trust's management regulation and an indication of the law applicable to the trust;

(iv) Registration and fees - MFTZ offshore trusts must be registered (however, the identification of the settlor and beneficiary is secret and can only be disclosed under a Court order) and its incorporation and registration is subject to the payment of an annual fee;

(v) Trust companies and branches - the incorporation and operation of trust branches or trust companies within the MFTZ is also allowed - provided that there is authorisation from the Madeiran Regional Government (*Governo Regional da Madeira*) and subject to the payment of an incorporation fee and an annual operation fee;

(vi) Tax benefits and exemptions - trusts and trust branches and companies enjoy the following benefits/tax exemptions:

(a) Trusts are exempt from corporation or individual income tax with respect to income arising from operations carried out with entities established within the MFTZ or with non-resident entities (whether located within the EU or not) without a permanent establishment in Portugal;

(b) The interest paid in respect of loans made by trusts and trust companies or branches is also exempt from corporation tax, provided that such loans were intended for investing within the MFTZ, or to support the trust or trust branch or company's regular operation, and the grantor is a non-resident entity;

(c) Income paid by trust branches or companies to clients established in the MFTZ or residing outside Portugal are exempt from corporation or individual income tax;

(d) Repatriation of invested capital and profits, transfer of funding for trade operations and funding imports are unrestricted.

(vii) Restriction on offshore trust activities - MFTZ trusts, trust companies or trust branches are not allowed to undertake financial activities.

11.4.2. Financial Services

11.4.2.1. Incorporation and Operation of Credit Institutions, Financial Companies or Insurance Companies or Branches thereof in the MFTZ

Decree-Law 10/94 of 13th January 1994 allowed the incorporation and operation of credit institutions (banks, investment companies, leasing companies, factoring companies, etc.), financial companies (dealers, brokers, investment fund managing companies, venture capital companies, etc.) and insurance or reinsurance companies, as well as the incorporation and operation of branches of such companies, in the MFTZ.

However, the Decree-Law 163/2003 of 24th July 2003 excludes from the new regime, all financial and insurance intermediary activities, financial and insurance ancillary activities and all " intra-group services" (coordination, accounting and distribution centres).

Taking into consideration the new regime, from 1st January 2001, financial companies engaging in such activities can no longer obtain new licenses. However entities licensed prior to 31st December 2000 may continue until 2011.

11.4.2.2. Specific Tax Benefits applicable to Credit Institutions, Financial Companies and Insurance Companies Operating in the MFTZ

Credit institutions, financial companies and insurance companies authorised to operate in the MTFZ in 2000 or before benefit from the following tax exemptions, until 2011:

a) Credit institutions and financial companies- ull exemption from corporation/individual income tax in respect of income arising from operations carried out within the MFTZ, provided that these operations only involve non-resident entities (and the latter are not subsidiaries of, or controlled in any form by, credit institutions residing in Portugal but outside the MFTZ).

b) Investment fund managing companies - full exemption from corporation/individual income tax in respect of income arising from the management of funds, at least 90% of whose assets are invested outside Portugal and whose units were acquired by non-resident entities only.

c) Insurance companies - full exemption from corporation/individual income tax, provided they operate only within the MFTZ or with non-resident entities (non-Life Insurance) or with non-residents only (life assurance).

11.4.3. The Industrial Free Trade Zone

Manufacturing businesses licensed to operate in the Madeira Industrial Free Trade Zone (MIFTZ) benefit, *inter alia*, from the following tax exemptions:

a) Full exemption, until 2011, from corporation and/or individual income tax on profits and dividends.

The corporation tax regime and the specific eligibility criteria that companies have to meet to benefit from the new reduced rates, are described above as per point 11.3.

However plants can benefit from a 50% reduction in their corporation tax rates, if they comply with two of the following conditions:
i) Develop the region's economy by technological innovation projects.
ii) Diversify the region's economy

iii) Introduce highly qualified employment opportunities in the region

iv) Improve environnemental conditions

v) Create and maintain a minimum of 15 jobs for at least 5 years.

b) Full exemption from tax due on the transfer of Real Estate Property ("IMT") within the MIFTZ by manufacturing businesses for their premises,

c) Full exemption of import duties on certain categories of raw materials to be processed at facilities located in the MIFTZ, pursuant to Council Regulation (EC) 22/96 of 22nd January 1996 and Commission Regulation (EC) 1482/97 of 28th July 1997.

11.4.4. - International Shipping Register (MAR)

A wide range of tax and financial incentives are available to shipping companies duly incorporated and licensed to operate within the legal framework of the Madeira Free Trade Zone.

The International Shipping Registry of Madeira (known as 'MAR') is the most recent cornerstone of the Madeira International Business Centre (a free trade zone created by Decree-Law 500/80, of 20th October 1980, managed and administered by SDM - Sociedade de Desenvolvimento da Madeira, S.A., a privately operated company that has the full support of the Autonomous Region of Madeira). MAR was created by Decree-Law 96/89 in 1989, and today the Registry is at the forefront of modern shipping legislation.

MAR's purpose is to register all acts and contracts which relate to commercial ships, fixed or floating platforms/installations, as well as leisure boats. MAR operates a high standard registration system which has introduced rigorous measures to assure an effective monitoring systems for all vessels registered. Consequently, MAR is not a register that merely awards flags of convenience indiscriminately. It is also responsible for the technical inspection of ships in general and the undertaking of any other acts inherent to registration obligations, such as: ship inspections, sign call attribution, ship certification, registration of the crew, issuing, validation and control of on-board documents, and many others.

Following a number of initiatives to promote quality shipping and eliminate the competitive distortion caused by the existence of the flag of convenience system, MAR has sought to prevent registration of sub-standard owners/operators looking for a 'suitable' flag of convenience. Indeed, the first technical inspection is always conducted by MAR. Only the subsequent annual inspections are delegated to internationally approved Classification Societies.

This is probably the reason why MAR has only registered 162 ships, when it could have easily reached more than 1000 registrations.

Recently, the legal framework that regulates ownership and crew registration has been amended in order to further enhance the advantages of the shipping register of Madeira, whilst adapting it to a new market reality, in which the former requirements that at least 80% of the crew, as well as the captain, must be EU nationals, have proved to be difficult to meet. These amendments will be described below.

11.4.4.1. - Important Aspects of the Madeiran Register

1) Entities able to Register:

1.1 Those whose purpose is that of maritime transportation of persons and goods. Applicants may be companies or other forms of partnerships, branches, agencies or legal representatives, licensed or not to operate in the legal framework of Madeira's International Business Centre.

1.2 Owners of yachts.

NB: Fishing vessels are not allowed to register at the Shipping Register of Madeira.

2) How to Register:

The information and documentation to be submitted to the Technical Commission of MAR varies depending on whether the registration is temporary or permanent. If the registration is permanent, the name of the ship will be submitted together with two alternative names, and the original Bill of Sale. If the registration is temporary, a certified copy of the bareboat chartering contract shall be submitted.

The law has established provisional registration for a maximum of 30 days, in order to facilitate permanent registration at the end of that period. The registration process is exempt from any form of taxation.

3) The Purchase and Sale of Ships:

This type of operation is not subject to any prior authorization. The sale becomes effective through a Bill of Sale.

4) Classification Societies:

Annual surveys, carried out to ensure compliance with internationally agreed standards, including safety regulations, are undertaken by MAR surveyors or by surveyors of Classification Societies recognised by the Ministry responsible for Maritime Affairs (the respective certificates are subsequently issued) The following Classification Societies are authorised to undertake surveys:

* Lloyd's Register of Shipping (LRS);
* Bureau Veritas (BV);
* Det Norske Veritas (DNV);
* Registro Italiano Navale (RINA);
* American Bureau of Shipping (ABS);
* Germanischer Lloyd (GL);
* Rinave Portuguesa (RINAVE);

Other classification societies may in the future be recognized by the Portuguese government.

5) Verification of Crew and their Tax Liability:

- Any income received by the crew of ships registered at MAR is exempt from any form of taxation (8 Art. 33 – Decree-Law 215/89, of 1st July 1989, as amended by Decree-Law 198/2001, of 3rd July 2001).

- The objective of the Register's technical commission in assessing crew composition and minimum crew requirements is to guarantee safety and the preservation of the quality of life on board and at sea. However, even though the Decree-Law 248/2002 states that the captain and 50% of the crew must be nationals of EU member states or of PALOP countries (Official Portuguese Speaking Countries), exceptions in certain special circumstances may be granted. This last proviso takes into account the shortage of captains and crew from EU member-states, allowing a larger number of non-EU nationals, for instance, citizens of Eastern European countries to become part of these crews.

In fact, applicants may propose the crew composition of their ship, according to the characteristics of the ship and International Conventions.

These crew requirements do not apply to yachts.

Crew members and their respective employers are not obliged to pay social security taxes levied under the normal Portuguese system and may opt for voluntary or private schemes.

6) Tax Benefits and Exemptions:

All tax benefits and exemptions applicable within the legal framework of Madeira's International Business Centre ('the Centre' or 'IBC') are extended to ship owners registered at MAR.

Until 2011, no corporation tax is due on profits made by operators of ships flying the Portuguese flag operating in international waters, registered until 31st December 2002. The same applies to profits made by ships owned by companies licensed to operate under the free trade zone legislation but flying a foreign flag. However, corporation tax is levied on income earned by owners of ships that carry cargo and passengers between national ports, at a rate of 25%. No capital gains tax is due on profits made on the sale of a ship or by the transfer of the shares of the company which owns the ship, provided that the shares sold are owned by a non-resident entity.

Ship owners will also benefit from an exemption from municipal property taxes until 2011.

Moreover, no withholding tax, corporation or individual income taxes are payable on dividends and interest on shareholder's loans.

Ship owners are also exempt from transfer tax on all transfers of shares or other forms of shareholding of companies operating exclusively in the Centre and on the acquisition of real estate for the purpose of setting up in the Centre.

Exemption from stamp tax and stamp duties on any documents or contracts signed by companies operating in Madeira's IBC may also be granted.

In addition, there are some VAT related advantages for vessels owned by companies licensed to operate under the Free Trade Zone legislation.

Since 1993, a leisure boat cannot remain in European Union waters for more than six months in any one year, unless it can prove that VAT has been paid on the yacht in one member state. A boat purchased by a company licensed to operate under the Free Trade Zone legislation of Madeira would automatically pay VAT so it would not fall foul of the six months rule.

A company licensed to operate under the Free Trade Zone legislation of Madeira pays VAT at a rate of 13% on the purchase of a vessel. The comparable rate in most other European Union jurisdictions is 17.5%.

If the ship is owned by a Madeira company, VAT is only due for the purchase of the vessel, since transportation of goods and passengers within the EU, as well as imports and transfers of goods to Free Trade Zones, are VAT exempt. In a number of other EU member states and dependent territories, tax-privileged companies which own vessels cannot register for VAT in the EU with resulting disadvantages when it comes to subsequent re-sale or transfer of the vessel within the EU.

Other tax advantages may be available through the implementation of double taxation treaties ratified by Portugal. As the members of the Free Trade Zone of Madeira are Portuguese companies with their head offices and central management in Portugal they are, therefore, subject to the same tax regime advantages applicable to all companies domiciled in Portugal, although they are temporarily exempt from taxation.

7) International Treaties

Portugal has ratified or signed approximately forty international treaties and agreements, not to mention double taxation agreements, including the following:

• Law of the Sea Convention, 1982 (UNCLOS)

157

- International Convention for the Safety of Life at Sea, 1974 (SOLAS)

- International Convention for the Prevention of Pollution from Ships, 1973 (MARPOL)

- International Convention on Maritime Search and Rescue, 1979 (SAR)

- International Convention on Oil Pollution Preparedness, Response and Co-operation, 1990 (OPRC)

- Lisbon Agreement: Cooperation Agreement for the Protection of the Coasts and the Northeast Atlantic against Pollution, 1990.

11.4.4.2. Legal Requirements

- Access Requirements

1-   All commercial vessels that operate in the marine environment including fixed or floating oil rig platforms.

2-   Registration Requirements.

2.1. Applications for permanent registration should be submitted together with the following documents and information:

- Purchase certificate of the vessel;
- Name of the vessel's owner;
- Intended name of the vessel and two alternative names;
- Owner and/or operator's contracts, mortgages or other charges on the vessels;
- Applications for the attribution of a call sign, as well as a description of communication equipment together with a copy of the last radio station licence issued by the Administration of the previous register;
- Vessel's tonnage measurement in accordance with the International Convention on Tonnage Measurement of Ships, 1969.
- Vessel's characteristics and propulsion system

- Construction shipyard of the vessel and year of construction;
- Name of Classification Society;
- Copies of the vessel's certificates;
- Name of the entity responsible for the payment of radio-communication accounts recognised by the Portuguese Administration;
- Crew's individual employment agreements;
- Ship's manning duly justified;
- Declaration (duly authenticated), issued by the competent authorities of the previous register, certifying that the applicant has asked for cancellation of registration;
- Subsequent immediate presentation of the Cancellation Certificate to MAR;
- General layout of the vessel;
- Safety layout. Fire extinguishing and rescue means;
- Stability Certificate approved by the Classification Society.

2.2.   Applications for temporary registration should be submitted together with the following documents and information:

- Original or notarised copy of the bareboat chartered contract;
- Operator's name;
- Vessel's name;
- Declaration of the vessel's owner authorizing temporary registration in MAR;
- Declaration of the competent authorities of the country where the vessel's ownership is registered authorizing temporary registration in MAR;
- Licence application containing the above-mentioned items.

3-   The registration of a vessel in MAR may be carried out whether companies are licensed to operate within the legal framework of Madeira's International Business Centre (IBC) or not, in contrast to the situation in Cyprus or Malta, for example, where the registration of vessels may only be carried out by licensed companies.

- If a ship owner wishes to register a vessel through a company licensed to operate within the legal ambit of Madeira's IBC, a licence application must be presented to the Regional Secretary for Planning and Finance (through this licence, the company will benefit from all the tax incentives granted within the scope of Madeira's IBC. It will pay for application and annual fees).

Shipping companies, duly licensed to operate within the legal framework of Madeira's IBC, will not be subject to some of the usual requirements, such as:

- Minimum Share Capital;
- Citizenship requirements relating to members of the Board of Directors or Management;
- Head offices in Madeira;
- Any registration or notaries fees in the process of incorporation and registration.

Furthermore, there are other advantages offered by the Shipping Register of Madeira to entities registering after 1st January 2003, such as the following:

- Reduced Corporation Tax Rates of 1% to 3%;
- Double Taxation Agreements;
- No withholding tax on dividends; and
- No capital gains tax on the transfer of ships.

If the company does not have its head offices in Madeira, it must nevertheless have a local branch, delegation, agency or any other appropriate form of representation. Such a branch or other must be able to maintain a legal relationship with the State Authorities and third parties, as well as to receive notifications/summons.

If a ship owner chooses to register the vessel through a shipping company not licensed to operate within the legal scope of Madeira's IBC and if this company does not have its head offices in Madeira, it must have a permanent representation in Madeira with all necessary powers.

11.4. - Other Tax Benefits and Exemptions applicable to the MFTZ

11.4.1. - Specific Tax Benefits (other than Income Tax Exemptions)

Apart from the corporation and/or individual income tax exemptions described in preceding sections, entities operating in the MFTZ enjoy an array of financial and tax benefits:

(a) No restriction applies on foreign entities licensed to operate within the MFTZ as regards the repatriation of invested capital and profits, transfer of funding for trade operations and funding of imports;

(b) Full exemption from tax payable on the transfer of Real Estate Properties ("IMT") in respect of immovable assets acquired to serve as their premises;

(c) Exemption from corporation or individual income tax on capital gains arising from the sale of construction land kept as reserve;

(d) Exemption from Municipality Tax on Immovable Assets (*"IMI"*) and from all local taxes and surtaxes;

(e) Exemption from stamp duty with regard to all books, papers, documents, contracts covered by the Stamp Duty Code, except where they relate to operations carried out with entities residing in Portugal but outside the MFTZ or non-resident entities with a permanent establishment in Portugal.

11.4.2. VAT Rules applicable to the MFTZ

Transactions occurring on the Island of Madeira are subject to value-added tax at reduced rates (4%, 8% and 13%), which makes the Island of Madeira the most favourable area in Europe as far as VAT is concerned.

11.4.3. Double Taxation Treaties

The tax exemptions and benefits described in the preceding sections can be further complemented with the double taxation treaties entered into by Portugal, which fully apply in MFTZ, as per chart twelve at chapter 13.

PUBLIC PROCUREMENT

CHAPTER 12

12.1. Introduction

The award of supply, service or public works contracts by state, regional or local authorities, or by entities governed by public law, must comply with national, European Union and international regulations. These are instrumental in ensuring transparency in award procedures, as well as equitable competitive conditions for potential bidders and good use of public funds.

The purpose of this chapter is to provide for a brief overview of public procurement regulations applying in Portugal.

12.2. European Union Legal Framework

Opening public procurement to competition is a key European Union policy tool for implementing the single market, thus stimulating Europe-wide competition and obtaining an effective allocation of public monies as well as improving quality standards and cost effectiveness.

The main EU rules on public procurement are:
- Council Directive 93/38/EEC of 14th June 1993, coordinating the procurement procedures of entities operating in the water, energy, transport and telecommunications sectors, as amended by Council Directive 98/4/EEC of 16th February 1998 and by Commission Directive 2001/78/EC of 13th September 2001 (the "utilities" directive);
- Council Directives 92/50/EEC, 93/36/EEC and 93/37/EEC, relating to the coordination of procedures for the award of, respectively, contracts for public services, public supplies and public works contracts, as amended by Council and European Parliament Directive 97/52/EC of 13th October 1997 and by Commission Directive 2001/78/EC of 13th September 2001 (the "Services", "Supplies" and "Works" directives).
- Commission Recommendation 96/527/EC of 30th July 1996, on the use of the Common Procurement Vocabulary (CPV) for describing the subject matter of public contracts;
- Council Directives 89/665/EEC of 21st December 1989 and 92/13/EEC of 25th February 1992, on the coordination of the laws, regulations and administrative provisions relating to the application of, respectively, review procedures to the award of public supply and public works contracts and of Community rules on the procurement procedures of entities operating in the water, energy, transport and telecommunications sectors (also known as the "remedies directives").

The 1997/98 amendments to the abovementioned directives incorporate the resolutions contained in the Government Procurement Agreement (GPA) concluded during the Uruguay Round multilateral negotiations by the Council on behalf of the Community (Decision 94/800/EEC of 22nd December 1994), effective 1 January 1996.

The GPA creates rights for suppliers, contractors and service providers of third countries, which have signed the agreement: Canada, South Korea, USA, Israel, Japan, Liechtenstein, Norway, Singapore, Switzerland and Hong Kong.

The European Parliament ("EP") is now discussing a Commission proposal on extensive amendments to the "Services", "Supplies" and "Works" directives as well as to the "Utilities Directive", intended to simplify the said directives in order to further stimulate public procurement within the EU and, with regard to the "Utilities Directive", to update it in view of the implementation of the final stage of the liberalisation of the water, energy, transport and telecommunications sectors. The EP is also discussing a proposal for an EP and Council regulation, under which the CPV would become mandatory in public procurement thus providing for a uniform public procurement "language" that would further facilitate EU-wide procurement procedures.

12.3. Public Procurement in the Water, Energy, Transport and Telecommunications Sectors

The so-called "Utilities Directive" was implemented in Portugal by Decree-Law 223/2001 of 9th August 2001.

12.3.1. Scope of Decree-Law 223/2001 of 9th August 2001

Decree-Law 223/2001, as amended by Decree-Law 245/2003 of 7th October 2003 that implements the European Commission's Directive 2001/78/CE of 13th September 2001, applies to public contracts awarded by state, regional or local authorities as well as to public companies in which state authorities are major shareholders or which hold public concessions, whose value (without VAT) is equal to, or over the following thresholds:

(i) Contracts awarded within the telecommunications sector:

- Public works contracts: 5,000,000 euros;

- Supply or service contracts: 600,000 euros.

(ii) Contracts awarded within the water, electricity and urban transport (including railways) sectors:

- Public works contracts: 5,000,000 Special Drawing Rights (SDE)/ 7,100,000 euros;

- Supply or service contracts within the CCP nomenclature (except research and development and telecommunications services): 400,000 SDE /568,000 euros.

- Other supply or service contracts: 400,000 euros.

(iii) Contracts awarded within the natural gas, oil, coal, and railway sectors:

- Public works contracts: 5,000,000 euros;

- Supply or service contracts: 400,000 euros.

Upon awarding public contracts whose value is under these thresholds, contracting authorities can choose between applying Decree-Law 223/2001 of 9th August 2001 and Decree-Laws 197/99 of 8th June 1999 and 59/99 of 2nd March 1999, all amended by Decree-Law 245/2003 of 7th October 2003, relating, respectively, to award procedures for public services/supplies contracts and to public works contracts.

12.3.2. Contract Award Procedures

Under Decree-Law 223/2001, contracts must be awarded by the following procedures:

- open procedures, whereby all interested entities may submit tenders;

- restricted procedures, whereby only those entities invited by the contracting authorities may submit tenders;

- negotiated procedures, whereby contracting authorities consult entities of their choice and negotiate the terms of the contract with one or more of them.

In restricted or negotiated procedures, contracting authorities can select tenderers through a pre-qualification system.

Contracting authorities must make known their intention to award a public contract through a public announcement.

12.4. Public Procurement in Other Sectors

12.4.1. Legal Framework

The "Supplies" and "Services" directives were first implemented by Decree-Law 55/95 of 29th March 1995, later revoked by Decree-Law 197/99, of 8th June 1999, as amended.

The "Works" directive was first implemented by Decree-Law 405/93, of 10th December 1993, revoked by Decree-Law 59/99, of 2nd March 1999.

12.4.2. Public Service Contracts and Supplies Contracts

12.4.2.1. Scope of Decree-Law 197/99 of 8th June 1999

The said Decree-Law, amended by Decree-Law 245/2003 of 7th October 2003, does not contain a definition for "Public Service Contract" or for "Public Supplies Contract". The former broadly means a contract for pecuniary interest concluded between a service provider and a contracting authority, while the latter is a contract for pecuniary interest concluded between a supplier and a contracting authority involving the purchase, lease, rental or hire purchase of products, with or without an option to buy them and the delivery of which may also include siting and installation operations.

Decree-Law 197/99 applies to contracts awarded by the state, or regional or local authorities as well as legal entities established for the specific purpose of meeting needs in the general interest, not having an industrial or commercial character, and financed, for the most part, by the state, or regional or local authorities, or subject to management supervision by such authorities, or having a managing or supervisory board, more than half of whose members are appointed by the same authorities.

Decree-Law 197/99 does not apply to public concession services, i.e., contracts whereby the state transfers the execution of a public service to an entity of its choice for pecuniary interest and for the right to manage the said service, awarded to private entities.

12.4.2.2. Contract Award Procedures

Contracting authorities may opt for one of the following types of procedures, in accordance with the value of the contract:

i)   Open or limited procedure (i.e., restricted to tenderers selected through a previous qualification system, where required by the sheer value or technical complexity of the service/supply to be rendered) - for contracts whose value is equal to, or over, 124,699.47 euros;

ii)   Negotiated procedure with the publication of a contract notice - for contracts whose value is under 124,699.47 euros;

iii) Negotiated procedure without the publication of a contract notice or restricted procedure (i.e. where only entities invited by the contracting authority may submit tenders) - for contracts under or equal to, or under, 74,819.68 euros;

iv)   Private treaty, with prior consultation of:

-at least five candidates: for contracts whose value is equal to, or under, 49,879.79 euros;

-at least three candidates: for contracts whose value is equal to, or under, 24,939.89 euros;

-at least two candidates, for contracts whose value is equal to, or under, 12,469.95 euros;

v)   Private treaty without prior consultation, for contracts whose value is equal to, or under 4,987.98 euros.

12.4.3. Public Works Contracts

12.4.3.1. Scope of Decree-Law 59/99 of 2nd March 1999

As amended by Law 163/99 of 14th September 1999, Decree-Law 159/2000 of 27th July 2000 and more recently by Decree-Law 245/2003 of 7th October 2003.

Public works contracts are contracts for pecuniary interest concluded between a contractor and a contracting authority, whose object is building, rebuilding, expanding, repairing, refurbishing and/or demolishing immovable assets, such works being sufficient in themselves to fulfil an economic and technical function.

Contracting authorities for the purposes of Decree-Law are the state, regional or local authorities, and legal entities in which the state is the sole or major shareholder, as well as public service concessionaires, wherever these wish to award a contract whose value is higher than the thresholds set out in Directive 93/37/EC.

12.4.3.2. Contract Award Procedures

Contracting authorities can execute public works by themselves or attribute such execution to private entities by means of a public concession agreement or a public works contract. While the former must be awarded through an open procedure, the latter can be awarded through on the following procedures:

i)   Open or restricted procedure (where only tenderers invited or selected by the contracting authority through a pre-qualification procedure may submit tenders) with the publication of a contract notice - both apply to all public works contracts;

ii)   Restricted procedure without the publication of a contract notice - for contracts whose value is under 249,398.95 euros;

iii) Negotiated procedure, with or without the publication of a contract notice - for contracts under or equal to, or under, 39,903.83 euros;

iv) Private treaty, with prior consultation with three candidates at least - for contracts whose value is equal to, or under, 24,939.89 euros;

v)   Private treaty without any prior consultation, for contracts whose value is under 4987,98 euros.

PORTUGUESE TAX SYSTEM

CHAPTER 13

13.1. Introduction

The Portuguese Tax System currently in force was first implemented in the mid-1980s in order to attune Portuguese tax legislation with the various directives concerning the harmonisation of the European Tax System adopted within the European Community.

The Portuguese Tax System is hereby analysed in light of the latest reforms introduced by Law 30-G/2000 of 29th December 2000, Decree-Laws 198/2001 of 3rd July 2001 and 221/2001 of 7th August 2001 and Law 32-B/2002 of 30th December 2002 up to Decree-Law 107-B/ 2003 of 31st December 2003.

13.2. Principal Taxes

The main taxes are:

i)   Tax on the Income of Individuals (" Imposto sobre o Rendimento das Pessoas Singulares" - IRS) is regulated by the Individual Income Tax Code, as enacted by Decree-Law 442-A/88 of 30th November 1988, as amended.

ii)   Tax on the Income of Corporate Entities ("Imposto sobre o Rendimento das Pessoas Colectivas" - IRC) is regulated by the Corporation Tax Code, as enacted by Decree-Law 442-B/88 of 30th November 1988, as amended.

iii)   Value Added TAX ("Imposto sobre o Valor Acrescentado" – IVA) is regulated by the Value Added Tax Code, as enacted by Decree–Law 394-B/84 of 26th December 1984, as amended.

iv)   Annual Tax on Real Estate Properties ("Imposto Municipal sobre Imóveis " -IMI), is regulated by the "IMI" Code, as enacted by Decree-Law 287/2003 of 12th November 2003.

v) Municipal Tax on the Transfer of Real Estate Properties ("Imposto Municipal sobre as Transmissões Onerosas de Imóveis " - IMT), is regulated by the "IMT" Code, as enacted by Decree-Law 287/2003 of 12th November 2003

vi) Stamp duty ("Imposto de Selo") is regulated by Law 150/1999 of 11th September 1999 (Stamp Duty Code), as amended.

13.3. Individual Income Tax (IRS)

13.3.1. Scope of Taxation

Individual Income Tax is due on the worldwide income received by individuals residing in Portugal as well as on the income received or deemed to have been received in Portugal by non-resident individuals.

13.3.1.1. Concept of Residence- Article 16 of IRS Code

The following individuals are deemed to be resident in Portugal with respect to the year in which the taxable income was obtained:

a) Individuals who spend more than 183 days consecutively or non consecutively in Portugal or remain there for a lesser period but keep a residence in the same country on 31st December of the same year that demonstrates the intention of maintaining a regular domicile there.

b) Crewmembers of vessels or aircraft used by entities with head offices or effective place of management in Portugal, if the former hold such a capacity as of 31st December of the same year.

c) Individuals who, although being abroad, are employed by the Portuguese State.

d) Members of the same family unit if the responsible member of the family is a Portuguese resident.

13.3.1.2. Concept of Income deemed to have been received in Portugal

The following categories of income are deemed to have been received in Portugal:

(i)   Income arising from activities performed therein;

(ii)   Labour earnings arising from activities carried out in Portugal or those paid by a resident entity;

(iii)   Income arising from directors' remuneration paid by a resident company;

(iv)   Income arising from employment aboard an aircraft or a vessel, if the employer is a resident entity.

(v)   Income arising from payments made by an entity residing or with head offices, place of management or a permanent establishment, in Portugal in respect of:

- Intellectual or industrial property rights;

- The supply of know-how in the commercial, industrial or scientific fields;

- Commercial activities or supply of services arising from a permanent establishment located in Portugal or carried out within this territory, except for services related to transportation, communications or financial activities;

- Intermediation activities;

- Any other capital income;

(vi)   Income arising from property situated in Portuguese territory, including capital gains arising from the transfer thereof;

(vii)   Capital gains resulting from:

- The transfer of shares and securities of resident companies;

- The transfer of industrial or intellectual property rights if the vendor is not the original owner of such rights;

- Derivative financial instruments, if such gains are paid by a resident entity;

(viii) Gambling, lotteries or raffle prizes if paid by a resident entity;

(ix)   Income arising from pensions paid by a resident entity.

13.3.2. Categories of Taxable Income

Individual Income Tax applies to, and is due in accordance with, the categories of income set out in chart 1 below:

CHART ONE:

> Categories of income:
>
> A- Dependent work (covers all employment-related earnings and certain fringe benefits)
>
> B -Business Activities and Supply of Services (covers earnings arising from commercial or industrial activities and/or from the supply of services)
>
> E- Capital income (covers remuneration paid by way of interest on capital investments, loans or bank deposits as well as share dividends)
>
> F- Property income (covers income arising from property lease or rental)
>
> G- Capital and other gains (covers capital gains, compensation awards and gambling, lotteries or raffle prizes)
>
> H- Pensions (covers retirement and disability pensions)

13.3.3.Tax Assessment

Tax on individual income is assessed in four steps:

a)   Category-specific tax-deductible expenses are deducted from the gross income received within each category of income listed above in order to determine taxable income (TI) per category;

b)   Total Taxable Income (TTI) is then determined by adding up all categories of TI;

c)   Tax rates in force are then applied to TTI so as to determine the basic tax assessment (BTI);

d)   Final tax assessment, i.e., amount of income tax payable by taxpayer is determined by deducting from the BTI any pertinent expenses listed in the IRS Code (health and education expenses, tax credits arising from international

171

double taxation, amounts paid by way of tax withheld at source, among others).

13.3.3.1. Particular Methods of Tax Assessment of B-Category Income

The latest IRS reforms introduced a dual method for assessing income tax in respect of B-category (Business and Supply of Services Activities) income: "the simplified assessment method" and "the organised accounts method".

13.3.3.1.1. "Simplified Assessment System"

The "simplified assessment system" applies to.
a)   Individuals carrying out business activities whose sales are equal to, or under, 149,739.37 euros;
b)   Services providers whose profit is equal to, or under, 99,759.58 euros.

Under this system, B-category taxable income is determined through the application of a 0.20 coefficient to the sales or a 0.65 coefficient to the gross profits from supply of services (i.e., sales X 0.20 = taxable income or gross profits from supply of services X 0.65 = taxable income).
As a consequence, only the expenses as specified in item 13.3.3. d) above can be deducted from the taxable income.
The "simplified assessment system" applies to a minimum taxable income equal to € 3,125.00 (three thousand, one hundred and twenty five euros).

13.3.3.1.2. "Organised Accounts System"

This system applies to all individuals whose sales or supply of services profits exceed the limits specified above or who opt for such a system.

172

As a consequence, such individuals are required to keep complete accounts identical to those of corporate taxpayers. Their B-category income is determined through the application of the corporation tax Code provisions regarding the calculation of the taxable profit, where appropriate.

B-category specific deductible expenses (the salaries of employees, taxpayers' or taxpayers' employees' travel, meal and lodging expenses, leases on premises and/or equipment required for taxpayer's activity, *inter alia*) apply within this system, since they are regarded as activity-related costs.

13.3.4. Tax Rates

Tax is levied on world-wide income as per the chart below:

CHART TWO:

Taxable Income (Euros)	Rates (%)	
	Normal (A)	Average (B)
≤ 4,266.00	12	12.0000
> 4,266.00 ≤ 6,542.00	14	12.6777
> 6,542.00 ≤ 15,997.00	24	19.4333
> 15,997.00 ≤ 36,792.00	34	27.6667
> 36,792.00 ≤ 53,322.00	38	30.8700
> 53,322.00	40	-

If the taxable income (TI) is higher than 4,266 euros, the rates contained in column B shall apply; however, the fraction of TI that exceeds the lower limit of the applicable band is taxed according to the tax rates in column A applicable to the band immediately above.

13.3.4.1. Withholding Tax Rates

Withholding Tax is applicable on Individual Income as specified below.

13.3.4.1.1. Withholding Tax on A-Category (Dependent Work) Income

There are two distinctive sets of withholding tax rates for A-category income:

a)   Withholding tax rates on entirely variable remunerations. These are deducted from each payment and determined in accordance with the total yearly amount of such remunerations as estimated at the beginning of the year, as per chart three below:

CHART THREE

Remuneration (euros)	Tax rate (%)
up to 4,586.00	0
From 4,586.00 up to 5,418.00	2
From 5,418.00 up to 6,425.00	4
From 6,425.00 up to 7,982.00	6
From 7,982.00 up to 9,662.00	8
From 9,662.00 up to 11,166.00	10
From 11,166.00 up to 12,792.00	12
From 12,792.00 up to 16,034.00	15
From 16,034.00 up to 20,838.00	18
From 20,838.00 up to 26,384.00	21
From 26,384.00 up to 36,056.00	24
From 36,056.00 up to 47,627.00	27

From 47,627.00 up to 79,381.00	30
From 79,381.00 up to 119,095.00	33
From 119,095.00 up to 198,534.00	36
Over 198,534.00	38

b) Withholding tax rates on fixed or partially fixed remunerations, which are deducted from the remunerations paid in accordance with a set of tables published annually by the tax authorities. The table of withholding tax rates for unwed taxpayers without children for 2003 is set out in chart four below:

CHART FOUR

Monthly Remuneration (Euros) / Tax Rates (%)					
Up to 430.07	0.0%	Up to 912.06	10.5%	Up to 2,053.13	21.5%
Up to 434.43	0.5%	Up to 980.36	11.5%	Up to 2,306.25	22.5%
Up to 438.89	1.5%	Up to 1,060.72	12.5%	Up to 2,627.68	23.5%
Up to 472.16	2.5%	Up to 1,157.14	13.5%	Up to 3,057.60	24.5%
Up to 494.20	3.5%	Up to 1,273.66	14.5%	Up to 3,459.38	25.5%
Up to 542.42	4.5%	Up to 1,386.17	15.5%	Up to 3,861.17	26.5%
Up to 602.69	5.5%	Up to 1,466.53	16.5%	Up to 4,367.43	27.5%
Up to 679.02	6.5%	Up to 1,550.91	17.5%	Up to 5,030.36	28.5%
Up to 747.32	7.5%	Up to 1,647.33	18.5%	Up to 5,930.36	29.5%
Up to 795.54	8.5%	Up to 1,759.83	19.5%	Up to 7,220.10	30.5%
Up to 847.78	9.5%	Up to 1,884.38	20.5%	Over 7,220.10	31.5%

13.3.4.1.2. Withholding Tax on other Income Categories

Withholding tax on other categories of income than A-category is collected as per chart five below:

WITHHOLDING TAX - CHART FIVE

Types of Income		Tax Rates (%)	
		Residents	Non Residents
A category	Dependent Work	See item 13.3.4.1.1.b)	25
B category	Supply of services in general	10	25
	Supply of Services within liberal professions	20	25
	Royalties (if received by original owner)	15	15
	Technical Assistance	10	15
E category	Share dividends	15	15
	Interest on bank deposits	20	20
	Public debt	20	-
	Income arising from swap operations, assignment of credits, securities for portfolio accounts with guaranty of price and other similar operations	20	20
	Redemption of life insurance policies	20	20
	Interest on the lease of agricultural or industrial equipment	15	15
	Share in a liquidated company's assets	15	25
	Other capital income	15	20

F category	Property income	15	15
G category	Compensations for moral damages, except those arising from court decisions, arbitration or settlement agreements	15	15
	Amounts arising from non-competition obligations	15	15
	Raffles, contests and lotto prizes	35	35
	Lottery, bingo and sports gambling prizes	25	25
H category	Pensions	*	25

*Withholding tax rates for pensions received by resident individuals are determined in a table published yearly by the tax authorities.

13.4. Corporation Tax (IRC)

Corporation tax is regulated by the corporation tax code (IRC Code), as enacted by Decree-Law 442-B/88 of 30th November 1988, with subsequent amendments, and applies to income and capital gains earned by the entities set out in item 13.4.1.1. below.

13.4.1. Scope of Taxation

Under applicable provisions of the IRC Code the following entities are subject to Portuguese corporation tax:

-Companies and other legal entities with their registered office or a *place of effective management*[1] in Portugal whose main activities are carried out in the commercial, industrial, or agricultural fields.

---

[1] In the U.K. please see equivalent concept defined as Central Management and Control. This concept is applied to determine the residence of a company for taxation purposes, the

-Companies and other legal entities with head offices or a *place of effective management* in Portugal, which carry out activities in the commercial, industrial or agricultural fields by way of ancillary activities.

-Legal entities, which do not have their registered office or a *place of effective management* in Portugal but have a branch or a permanent establishment in Portugal.

-Entities without either registered offices or an effective place of management or a permanent establishment in Portugal, which earn income and/or capital gains, deemed to arise from a Portuguese source.

13.4.1.1. Concept of Permanent Establishment

An entity is deemed to have a permanent establishment in Portugal whenever it engages in commercial, industrial or agricultural activities through:

(i)   Fixed premises located therein, namely a place of management, branch, office, factory or workshop or natural resource extraction site (mine or oil derrick) or a construction or assembly yard, if the construction or assembly yard lasts for more than six months;

(ii) An employee or an agent engaged *ad hoc* empowered to negotiate and conclude any contracts on behalf of and in the interest of that entity, except if such an agent is a self-employed or acting independently within his normal professional capacity.

13.4.1.2. Fiscal Transparency

Relevant provisions of the IRC Code stipulate that the taxable profits of entities with head offices or effective places of management in Portugal are directly attributable to the members or shareholders irrespective of dividend distribution and taxed according to the applicable rules either of the Individual Income Tax Code or of the corporation tax Code, where such entities are:

---

company being regarded as tax resident in the country in which central management and control of its affairs is exercised.

(i)   Companies incorporated under the form of Civil Companies with Commercial Capacity;

(ii)   Professional partnerships; or

(iii)   Civil companies constituted for the management of assets, whenever the majority of the share capital belongs either to a family group for more than 183 days or to a maximum five shareholders, none of which can be a legal entity governed by public law.

13.4.1.3. Period of Assessment

IRC is assessed over a period equal to a financial year, which matches the calendar year. However, a financial year other than the calendar one can be adopted by:

i)   Non-resident entities with a permanent establishment in Portugal, which must use the adopted financial year for a minimum five-year period;

ii)   Resident entities under permission by the Minister of Finance, if such adoption is justified by economic reasons.

13.4.2. Taxable Income

i) Companies and legal entities with head offices or an effective place of management in Portugal are subject to taxation on income arising on a word-wide basis.

ii) Companies and legal entities, which do not have their head offices or effective place of management in Portugal, but have a branch or permanent establishment in Portugal are subject to taxation on income and capital gains attributed to the activities of such a branch or permanent establishment.

iii) Companies and legal entities that neither have their head offices nor an effective place of management or permanent establishment in Portugal are subject to taxation on income deemed to have been received in Portugal.

179

13.4.3. Tax Assessment

A dual assessment method also applies in respect of corporation tax: the "simplified assessment method" and "the organised accounts method".

13.4.3.1. "Simplified Assessment System"

The simplified assessment system applies to resident entities whose main activity is of a commercial, industrial or agricultural nature and which have not opted for the "organised accounts system", provided that:
  a) They do not benefit from a special IRC taxation regime;
  b) They are not exempt from IRC;
  c) They are not legally required to have external account auditing;
  d) They have a total annual return lower than 149,639.37 euros.

Under this system, taxable income is determined through the application of 20 % to the sale value of goods and 45 % to all other types of income.

The taxable income hereby determined cannot be lower than €6,250.00 (six thousand, two hundred and fifty euros).

Entities whose taxable income is determined by this system cannot deduct any tax credits arising from double international taxation on income obtained outside Portugal.

13.4.3.2. "Organised Accounts System"

Under this system, taxable income is determined on the basis of net accounting profits, as adjusted for allowable expenses and any profits or gains that may be excluded from taxation as well as for tax credits arising from double international taxation on income obtained outside Portugal.

13.4.4. Corporation Tax (IRC) General Rates

IRC is levied as per chart 7 below:

CHART 7

Entities	Rate (%)
Resident entities or branches of non-resident entities whose main activity is of a commercial, industrial or agricultural nature	30 (a) 2003 25 (a) 2004
Resident entities whose main activity is not of a commercial, industrial or agricultural nature	20
Resident entities whose taxable income is assessed by means of the "simplified assessment system"	20 (a)
Non-resident entities without a permanent establishment in Portugal	25(b)

a) Plus a Municipal surcharge levied by many local tax authorities.

b) Except in the cases where a specific different rate is stipulated.

13.4.4.1. Withholding Tax on Certain Types of Income at Specific Rates

Certain types of corporation income are subject to withholding tax as per chart 8 below:

CHART 8

Types of Income	Tax Rates (%)	
	Residents	Non Residents
Royalties (if received by the original owner)	15	15
Technical Assistance	10	15
Provision of Services deemed to be made in Portugal, with the exception of transport, communications and financial activities	10	10
Share dividends	15	25
Interest on bank deposits	20	20
Government bonds	20	20
Income arising from swap operations, assignment of credits, securities for portfolio accounts with guaranty of price and other similar operations	20	20
Interest on the lease of agricultural or industrial equipment	15	15
Shares in a liquidated company's assets	15	25
Other capital income	15	20
Compensation for moral damages, except those arising from court decisions, arbitration or settlement agreements	15	15
Amounts arising from non-competition obligations	15	15

13.4.4.2. Payments on Account

With the perspective of drawing the date of payment of Corporation Tax nearer to the moment where income is earned, some companies are obliged to effect payments in advance.

The obligation to effect payments on account occurs in the following cases:

Taxpayers	Tax Payment
Resident companies whose main activity is of commercial, industrial or agricultural nature and non-resident entities with a permanent establishment.	Payments on account must be made in July, September and December. The remaining amount must be paid by the end of the legal time limit for submission of the IRC annual return.
Resident companies whose main activity is not of a commercial, industrial or agricultural nature.	Payment must be made by the end of the legal time limit for submission of the IRC annual return.
Non-resident entities without a permanent establishment.	Payment must be made by the end of the legal time limit for submission of the IRC annual return.

If the taxation period does not coincide with the civil year, payments on account should be made on the seventh, ninth and twelfth months of the corresponding taxation period and the annual IRC return should be submitted by the fifth month after the term of this period.

Payments on account are calculated upon the taxable income of the former year, after withholding tax, and shall correspond:

- To 75% of the aforesaid amount, divided in three equal instalments, for taxpayers whose turnover does not exceed €498,797.90;
- To 85% of the aforesaid amount, divided in three equal instalments, for taxpayers whose turnover does exceed €498,797.90;

Payments on account shall not take place whenever the payable tax for the period is less than € 199.52.

To avoid an eventual excessive payment on account, namely in case of the downsizing of the company's activities, if the taxpayer he realizes that the amount paid on account is higher than the payable tax, he is allowed to limit the payments or not to effect another payment. For that purpose, the taxpayer must send his local Tax Department a statement by the end of the legal time limit to effect the next payment on account.

13.4.4.3. Special Payments on Account

Besides payments on account to which article 97 of the IRC Code refers, IRC taxpayers, who are not under the "simplified assessment system" and whose main activity is of a commercial, industrial or agricultural nature, must effect a special payment on account in March[2] or, in two instalments to be paid in March and October of each year.

The amount of the abovementioned payment is 1% of the company's turnover in the previous year, or a minimum of € 1,250.00, where higher, this minimum amount will be increased by 20% of the difference, between the above mentioned minimum amount of 1,250.00 and the tax assessment obtained by the application of 1% to company's turnover, until a maximum amount of € 40,000.00.

The payments on account made in the previous year will be deducted from the aforementioned amount.

For purposes of calculation of the amount to pay, turnover is deemed to be the amount of sales effected and services provided. If the taxpayer is a bank, insurance company or any other financial entity, for which there is a specific accountancy plan, turnover will be replaced by interests, similar profits and commissions, according to the taxpayer's activity.

---

[2] The time limit for 2003 has been postponed to June.

For fuel, tobacco, vehicles subject to special tax, alcoholic beverages and spirits retail sectors, the following taxes can be deducted from the special payment on account:

a) Special tax on vehicles;
b) Special consumption taxes.

The following cases are not subject to special payments on account:

1. In the two first years of a company's operation;
2. By taxpayers totally exempt from IRC; and
3. By taxpayers involved in Special Recovery and Bankruptcy Proceedings.

Whenever the special taxation regime for groups of companies, special payments on account are due by each of the group's companies, including the controlling company, the latter should calculate the amount of special payment on account and effect the corresponding payment.

13.4.5. Thin Capitalisation Rules

Thin capitalisation rules, set out in the relevant provisions of the IRC Code mainly stipulate that whenever a loan made by a non-resident entity to a resident company, in which it holds a specific business interest, is deemed to impose excessive indebtedness on the said company, the interest paid on the part of the loan deemed to be excessive, is not tax-deductible.

a) A non-resident entity is deemed to hold a "specific business interest" in a resident company in the following situations:

(i) Where it has a 10% or higher holding in the share capital or voting rights of the said resident company;

(ii) Where the resident company is a subsidiary of the non-resident entity;

(iii)   Where the majority of the Board members of the non-resident entity are also Board members of the resident company;

(iv)   Wherever the resident company depends on the non-resident in respect of management decisions, price-fixing or market distribution, on account of the commercial, financial or legal relationship between them;

b)   A non-resident entity outside the abovementioned situations is also deemed to have a "specific business interest" in the resident company if the loan in question is secured or guaranteed by another company in which the lender holds a "specific business interest" as defined above;

A debt/capital ratio of 2:1 is deemed to be an excessive indebtedness for the purposes of thin capitalisation rules.

However, interest paid on the part of the loan can be deducted as costs. upon proof that a similar loan could have been granted by an independent entity.

If the loan is granted by an individual, any interest paid is subject to withholding tax at the following rates:

a)   Residents: 15%; should the interest rate be equal or higher than the LISBOR reference rate and paid interest will be subject to an autonomous taxation at a 20% rate.

b)   Non-Residents: 20%.

If the loan is granted by a pure holding company, under the circumstances foreseen in the IRC Code, interest paid will be exempt from withholding tax.

13.4.6. Specific Regime for Mergers, Demergers, Transfers of Assets and Exchange of Shareholdings

The IRC Code contains a specific taxation regime applicable to mergers, demergers, transfers of assets and exchanges of shares, thus incorporating Directive 90/434/EEC of the Council of 23rd July 1990, on the common system of taxation applicable to such operations.

13.4.6.1. Scope of the Regime

This specific taxation regime applies to:

a)   Resident companies with a turnover of more than EUR 149,639.37;

b)   Non-resident companies covered by Directive 90/434/EEC.

This regime is also applicable to mergers, demergers and transfers of assets concerning other entities than commercial companies. It does not apply, however, to operations, which involve the transfer of aircraft or ships to non-resident airlines or shipping operators or to operations whose purpose is to avoid taxation.

13.4.6.2. Specific Taxation for Mergers, Demergers and Transfers of Assets

For the purposes of assessing the taxable income of the companies subject to a merger, demerger or transfer of assets, the earnings resulting from the transfer of on-balance-sheet businesses as a consequence of the merger, demerger or transfer of assets, shall not be taken into consideration, nor shall the provisions concerning the transferred credits, stocks and obligations be considered as profits or earnings, provided that the above-referred operations relate:

(i)   To the transfer of on-balance-sheet assets allocated to a permanent establishment in Portugal (a) between resident companies; (b) between a resident company and a company resident in another European Union (EU) Member State, or (c) between EU-resident companies (either in the same or in different Member States), provided that the transferred on-balance-sheet businesses remain allocated to a permanent establishment located in Portugal and plays a part in generating its taxable income; or

(ii)   To the transfer of a permanent establishment located in the territory of another EU Member State, between Portuguese-resident companies.

This legal regime does not apply to the transfer of a permanent establishment located outside Portugal, from a resident company to another EU-resident company, the former only being entitled to deduct the tax payable in the territory where the establishment is located.

13.4.6.3. Transfer of Tax Losses

According to the applicable provisions of the IRC Code, the merged company's tax losses can be deducted from the profits of the new company or those of the merging company, under authorisation granted by the Finance Minister upon presentation of a plan to restructure or rationalise the applicant's activities.

This regime also applies to the following (adjusted where appropriate):

(i)   Demergers in which the demerged company is wound up;

(ii)   To transfers of assets which entail the transfer and subsequent extinction of a permanent establishment located in Portugal, to a resident company from a non-resident company covered by Directive 90/434/EEC;

(iii)   To the transfer of a permanent establishment located in Portugal carried out within a merger, demerger or transfer of assets and between EU-resident companies, provided that the transferred on-balance-sheet businesses remain allocated to a permanent establishment located in Portugal and play a part in generating its taxable income.

13.4.6.4. Transfer of Holdings to the Shareholders of Merged or Demerged Companies and Exchange of Shareholdings

Capital gains or losses arising from:

a) The transfer of holdings in a company resulting from a merger to the shareholders of the merged companies; or

b) The transfer of holdings in the companies resulting from a demerger to the shareholders of the demerged company; or

c) The transfer of holdings in the acquiring company to the shareholders of the acquired company in exchange for holdings in the acquired company are exempt from corporation tax, provided that the accounting par value of the new shareholding is identical to that of the shareholding in the merged, demerged or acquired company.

However, this exemption only applies to the exchange of holdings if:

a)   Both acquiring and acquired companies reside in Portugal, or in another EU Member State and comply with Directive 90/434/EEC; and

b)   The acquired company's shareholders are individuals or legal entities residing in an EU Member State.

As far as exchanges of holdings are concerned, the same exemption does not preclude taxation of cash payments made to the shareholders of the acquired company along with the transfer of holdings in the acquiring company. Should those shareholders already own holdings in the acquiring company, the holdings transferred as a result of the exchange must be registered in separate accounts from the former.

13.4.6.5. Capital Gains

According to the relevant provisions of the IRC Code, capital gains arising from mergers, demergers, transfers of assets or exchanges of holdings consist of the difference between the acquisition value of the transferred on-balance-sheet assets and the realisation value, which, in case of mergers and demergers, is the market value of the on-balance-businesses transferred within such operations.

13.5. Value Added Tax (VAT)

13.5.1. Payment of VAT

VAT is a general consumer tax payable by suppliers of goods and services, who charge it in every supply they make within their respective activities, and afterwards pay the respective amount to the Tax Authorities.

VAT is payable whenever a good is supplied or a service is provided. It is a tax on consumer expenditure therefore companies (where they are VAT registered and fully taxable) do not bear the final costs of VAT. They are able to charge VAT on the goods or services they supply (output VAT) and recover VAT on purchases (input VAT).

13.5.2. Exemptions

Internal transactions, imports and exports may be exempt from VAT in certain cases.

VAT exemptions usually disturb the normal functioning of the deductions mechanism, having an impact on the neutrality of the Value Added Tax.

Obviously, wherever a transaction is tax-exempt, the supplier does not charge VAT but, on the other hand, he cannot deduct the VAT he has borne on his acquisitions, since that deduction implies charging VAT on sales.

13.5.2.1.Internal Transactions

The following activities are tax-exempt from VAT:

a) Social or general interest activities, such as:

  i)   Health, medical and hospital care;

  ii)   Social security and assistance;

  iii)   Education and teaching;

  iv)   Vocational training;

  v)   Sports activities;

  vi)   Culture, sciences and art;

  vii)   Spiritual Assistance;

  viii) Collective defence of material and moral interests of the members of non-profit political, union, religious, humanitarian, patriotic, philanthropic, recreational, sports, cultural, civic and economic institutions;

  ix)   Exact reimbursement of the quota of expenses made by autonomous groups of people carrying out tax-exempt activities;

x)	Supply of food and drinks to employees;	
xi)	Activities of public broadcast companies, of a non-commercial nature.	

b)   Banking, financial, insurance and re-insurance operations;

c)   Rental and transfer of real estate;

d)   Agricultural production and provision of agricultural services;

e)   Other exemptions include the following:

     i)   Public postal services (except for telecommunications);

     ii)   Sale of postage and fiscal stamps;

     iii)   Public services of garbage collection;

     iv)   Services provided by funeral directors;

     v)   All activities subject to special game taxes;

     vi)   Sales of goods whose tax borne on their acquisition has not been deducted.

13.5.3. Exemption on Imports

The following import transactions are exempt from VAT:

a)   Transactions in of the following goods are VAT-exempt in Portugal;

     i)   Ships, aircraft, related integrated objects and sea fishery equipment;

     ii)   Human organs, milk and blood;

     iii)   Literary, scientific, technical, and artistic bibliographic work, imported by either their authors or heirs;

     iv)   Currencies and legal means of payment, except for bank notes and coins that do not have current use or have numismatic interest.

b)   Trade in goods on board ships or aircrafts engaged in international passenger transport;

c)   Fish caught by fishing companies;

d)   Gold imported by *Banco de Portugal*;

e)   Automobiles, tricycles and wheelchairs;

f)   Provision of services whose value is included in the taxable amount of the imports of the goods to which they refer to;

g)   Imported goods within the scope of international, diplomatic and consular relationships;

h)   Goods that have been granted duty-free entry;

i)   Audiovisual goods for educational, scientific and cultural purposes;

j)   Collector's items and works of art not meant for sale.

13.5.4. Exemption on Exports, Similar Transactions and International Transportations

Unlike the previous cases, exemptions on exports, similar transactions or international transportation do not affect the neutrality of the Value Added Tax.

Indeed, in these cases, although the seller/service provider does not charge VAT to the acquirer of his goods or services, the former still has the right to ask for the reimbursement of the VAT borne on his acquisitions.

The following activities are tax-exempt:

a)   Supply of goods meant for export or similar transactions;

b)   Provision of services related to the international trade of goods;

c)   Supply of goods and provision of services concerning ships, aircraft and their freight.

13.5.5. Value Added Tax – Rates

VAT is collected at the following tax rates:

CHART NINE

Rate	Portugal	Azores and Madeira
Reduced rate	5%	4%
Intermediate rate	12%	8%
General rate	19%	13%

13.5.6. Tax-deductible Expenses

Suppliers of goods and services are legally required to charge VAT and are allowed to deduct from the VAT they have charged, the amount of VAT included in the expenses they incurred within their respective activities as well as the amount of VAT included in imports.

However, some expenses are deemed to be personal or unrelated to the supplier's activities and therefore not VAT-deductible, such as fuel expenses (only 50% of these are deductible), business travel or lodging expenses, tourism vehicles acquisition and maintenance expenses.

13.5.7. VAT Regime for Intra-Community Transactions

Since 1993, intra-Community transactions of goods are taxable subject to special regulation.

Decree-Law 290/92, of 28th December 1992, implemented Directive 91/680/CEE, of 16th December 1991, which replaced the former definition of "import" by the new concept of "intra-Community transaction".

Since then, "import" means only the entry into the Community of goods that originate from non-Member States and territories which, despite being a part of the European Union, are non integrated into the Community's tax jurisdiction.

The concept of intra-Community transaction is a very broad one, which, for taxation purposes, must be applied restrictively. Therefore, according to article 1 of the VAT Regime for intra-Community transactions, only the intra-Community transactions that comply with the following conditions are taxable transactions:

     i) The vendor must be a VAT taxpayer;

ii) The acquirer must be a VAT taxpayer, a totally exempt taxpayer or a non-taxpayer legal person under an intra-Community transactions taxation regime;

iii) The goods must be sent or transported to Portugal from another Member State's territory.

13.5.7.1. Exemptions

Pursuant to the VAT Regime for intra-Community transactions, transactions made to another Member State will be exempt from taxation provided that the acquirer meets the following criteria:

> *i)* To be an individual or legal person duly registered for VAT taxation in another Member State;
>
> *ii)* To have used the corresponding fiscal identification number to effect the transaction;
>
> *iii)* To be covered by an intra-Community transaction of goods taxation regime in that Member State.

Intra-Community transactions of new vehicles and other means of transport will always be levied in the Member State of destination.

The transfer of a company's assets, by the taxpayer or by someone on his behalf to another Member State, is also tax exempt.

A similar situation occurs whenever a transfer of goods carried from Portugal to the armed forces of another Member State, which is a member of the North Atlantic Treaty Organization (NATO), takes place.

13.5.7.2. Rates

Rates applicable to intra-Community transactions are similar to those foreseen in article 18 of the VAT Code concerning transactions of similar goods.

13.5.7.3. Deductions

General rules of the VAT Regime for Intra-Community Transactions foresee the right to deduct the VAT borne on intra-Community acquisitions and similar transactions.

Generally, there are two necessary conditions to exercise the right to deduct VAT, namely the following:

a)   that the taxpayer has included the value of the acquisition and the amount of payable tax in his VAT return, and

b)   that he has the corresponding invoice.

However, in cases in which the taxpayer does not have an invoice, he can still deduct the corresponding VAT, if the value of the transaction is evidenced through an internal document.

13.6. Annual Tax on Real Estate Property (*"Imposto Municipal Sobre Imóveis"* - IMI)

13.6.1. Scope of Taxation

IMI has been in force since 1st December 2003 and is payable on the taxable value of real estate property (urban buildings as well as construction sites and rural land), in each municipality by the owner or beneficiary of the property as of 31st December of each year.

13.6.1.1.The Taxable Value

New real estate property will have their taxable value, known in Portugal as *"Valor Patrimonial,"* assessed in accordance with the criteria set out by the Annual Tax on Real Estate Property Code (CIMI).

The real estate properties built and registered before December 2003 will be reassessed under CIMI following a change in ownership or, if that does not occur, after 10 years.

The taxable value of urban properties, namely, residential, commercial, industrial and services shall result from the following formula:

Vt = Vc * A * CA* Cl * Cq * Cv

Vt = Taxable Value

Vc = The bare value of buildings equals the average cost of building per square meter plus the value of land assessed as 25% of building cost.

A = Construction area as calculated (1)

CA = The use of property factor: residential accommodation =1.00 Accommodation = 1.00; commercial = 1.2; inside garage = 0.40; outside parking = 0.08

Cl = Location factor: rural areas = 0.35; upmarket area = up to 3 but generally between 0.4 and 2.

Cq = Quality and comfort factor: between 0.5 e 1.7.

Cv = The age of the property factor: from 0.35 (80 years) to 1 (less than 3 years).

(1) The construction area is calculated according to the following formula :

$$A = Aa *Ab*Ac*Ad$$

Aa = represents the private rough area

Ab = represents the dependent rough areas

Ac = represents the free area up to the limit of the implantation area times two

Ad = represents the free area exceeding the abovementioned limit

13.6.1.1.1 Transitory Period

During a transitory period of five years counting from the date on which the code comes into force and until properties are revalued in accordance with the new criteria, values will be reassessed as follows:

13.6.1.1.1.1. Properties that are not rented

Since 31^{st}December 2003, the taxable value of urban properties has been corrected in line with the currency revaluation table and adjusted according to regional property market swings in Portugal.

A rate of up to 44.21 % prior to adjustment will be applied to the taxable value of properties at first registration.

The earliest point of reference is 1970.

13.6.1.1.1.2. Rented Properties

The taxable value of rented properties, or part thereof, will be corrected in accordance with their annual rental value multiplied by 12 in the event that this sum is lower than the reassessed value obtained for the property.

When properties are reassessed under the new criteria, the taxable value of rented properties cannot exceed the sum equivalent to 15 times the annual rent.

13.6.1.1.2. Tax Limit Increases

Thresholds will apply to limit tax increases in the transitory period. Increases in tax payable in the following year cannot exceed:

2004 = 60 €

2005 = 75 €

2006 = 90 €

2007 = 105 €

2008 = 120 €

These thresholds will not apply to properties re-assessed under CIMI, or to offshore companies.

13.6.2. IMI Tax Rates

The municipal tax rate is levied on the taxable value of each real estate property as determined by the municipal tax authorities, in accordance with the following rates:

i)   Rural land: 0.8%;
ii) Urban buildings: between 0.4% and 0.8%.
iii) New urban buildings valued according to CIMI : between 0.2% a
     0.5%.

13.6.2.1 Anti-avoidance Measures

Wherever the owner is resident or domiciled in a country or region considered as a "highly favourable tax system", as per table laid out in the governmental order of the Ministry of Finance, the applicable tax rate will be 5%.

13.6.3. IMI Exemption Chart

Urban buildings for residential use only, have IMI exemption, as per the following chart:

CHART TEN

Taxable value	Exemption period
<= 150 000.00 €	6 years
> 150 000.00 € <= 225 000.00 €	3 years

However this exemption is valid only twice for the same taxable person or tax household.

13.7. Municipal Tax on the Transfer of Real Estate Properties ("*Imposto Municipal sobre as Transmissões Onerosas de Imóveis*"- IMT)

13.7.1. Scope of Taxation

"IMT", has been in force since 1st January 2004 and is payable on the transfer of real estate properties and in the transfer of any rights *in rem*. As a rule, must be paid by the acquirer.

For purposes of the present tax, the provisions of the IMT Code identify certain acts and contracts where a transfer of real estate property is deemed to have taken place.

13.7.1.1 Urban Buildings / Rural Property

As regards urban buildings, IMT is levied on the price of the purchase set out in the deed or on the taxable value of the real estate property whichever is the higher.

As for rural properties, IMT is levied on their taxable value. It is worthwhile mentioning that the criteria used for determining the taxable value of urban buildings is substantially different from that of rural properties.

13.7.1.1.1 Concept of Property transfer for IMT purposes

A transfer of real estate property is deemed to have taken place in cases such as:
a)   If the signing of promissory contracts for the purchase and sale of properties gives rise to the transfer of their possession, except where the property is the purchaser's permanent main place of residence and the promissory contract does not comprise any of the situations targeted by the anti-avoidance measures as per point 13.7.1.1.2 bellow.

b) A rental agreement whereby the property becomes the property of the tenant upon settlement of all rental payments.

c) Leases or sub-leases for over 30 years including those resulting from an extension of the original contract.

13.7.1.1.2 For Anti-avoidance purposes IMT is also payable:

a) In cases where a Promissory Contract or an amendment thereto provides, that a buyer may assign his position to a third party.

b) On assignment of a contract as above.

c) On the issuance of an irrevocable Power of Attorney to sell either a property or shareholdings in a company holding a property.

d) On the issuance of an instrument, e.g. a company resolution, coupled with a delegation of powers for the sale of a particular property.

e) On the termination, or extension by mutual agreement of a promissory contract for the acquisition of property or exchange of property when 10 years have elapsed from the date of possession or transfer of right.

f) On exchanges of real estate property, on the difference of the respective values.

g) On the division of property ownership of an Estate, on the difference value between the inherited share and the remaining part of the property acquired through purchase.

h) On the sale of water and mining rights.

i) On the transfer of real estate property for purposes of paying up the share capital corresponding to a certain shareholding and on the allocation of real estate property to shareholders by virtue of a company's winding up.

j) On the acquisition of at least 75% of the share capital in a Limited quota company holding a real estate property.

13.7.1.2. Particular Methods of calculating IMT

In particular, IMT is chargeable:

a) On the transfer of a property given as payment for a loan, either on it's taxable value or, on the amount of the loan, whichever is the higher.

b) On the 'usufruct' (the right to enjoy the use and advantages of another's property) if it is transferred separately from the base value of a property or vice-versa. IMT is charged at a special rate, according to certain criteria laid out in a specific chart provided for in the IMT Code.

c) In respect of leases or subleases, on 20 times the annual rental value if equal to or greater than the patrimonial value.

d) In respect of shareholdings or the distribution of company's assets to shareholders, on the taxable value or the value given to the shareholding whichever is the higher.

e) On the assignment of a contractual position, on the amount paid by the purchaser to the vendor, or, by the assignee to the assignor, but the rate of tax will be that applicable to the total consideration under the contract.

13.7.1.3. When IMT is payable

As general rule IMT is payable before the signing of a deed of the promissory contract, assignment of the contractual position, the signing of a Power of attorney, and so on, i.e. before the taxable event takes place.

13.7.1.4 Transitory Regime

While the taxable value of the real estate properties is being re-assessed according to the new criteria set out in the relevant provisions of the new IMI Code, the existing taxable value of real estate properties is valid, but tax payers may be later subject to pay additional tax, if according to the new criteria, a higher value is reassessed.

13.7.2. Tax Rates

"IMT" is levied in accordance with the following rates:

i)   Rural property - 5%;

ii)   Urban buildings with no residential use and all other onerous transfers – 6.5%;

iii)   Urban buildings, or parts thereof, for residential use only - IMT is charged as per the following chart:

CHART ELEVEN

Transfer value (euros)	Tax rates (%)	
	Marginal	Average
≤ 80 000,00	0	0
> 81 000,00 ≤ 110 000,00	2	0.5455
> 110 000,00 ≤ 150 000,00	5	1.7333
> 150 000,00 ≤ 250 000,00	7	3.8400
> 250 000,00 ≤ 500 000,00	8	-
> 500 000,00	6 (single tax rate)	

If the transfer value is higher than 80, 000.00 euros, the average tax rate corresponding to the band within which that value is contained shall apply; however, the fraction of the transfer value that exceeds the lower limit of the said band is taxed according to the marginal tax rates applicable to the band immediately above.

13.7.2.1. Anti-avoidance Mesures

Wherever the acquirer is resident or domiciled in a country or region considered as a "highly favourable tax system", as per table laid out in governmental order of Ministry of Finance, the applicable tax rate will be 15%.

13.8. Stamp Duty

13.8.1. Scope of Taxation

Stamp duty is levied on a wide range of deeds, contracts, documents, titles, books, papers and financial operations, covering more than a hundred deeds, contracts and operations.

Stamp duty must be paid by the person with an economic interest in the deed or contract such as the buyer in a purchase contract, credit institutions or financing companies in financial operations.

13.8.2. Tax Exemptions

Stamp duty is not applicable when VAT is levied on the same operation.

Moreover, certain categories of deeds, contracts and financial operations are exempt from stamp duty, such as the following:

a)   Interest on loans granted for acquisition, construction, re-construction or improvement of residential buildings or parts thereof;

b) Loans, as well as interest and/or commissions charged thereon, granted by credit institutions, financing companies and venture capital companies to similar entities, provided that both grantor and grantee reside within the European Union (EU) or, if one of them is a non-EU resident, that they do not reside in a country deemed to be a "tax haven";

c) Financial operations, including interest charged thereon, between companies and their respective subsidiaries, provided that the former hold a minimum 10% holding in the latter for one year;

d) Incorporation and increase in share capital of pure holding companies (SGPS) and venture capital companies;

e) Guarantees granted to the State within the management of public debt with the sole purpose of covering the latter's credit exposure;

f) Documents, books, papers, contracts, operations, deeds and products in the tax-free trade areas of Madeira and of the Santa Maria Island (Azores), as per article 33, paragraph 11 of Decree-Law 215/89, of 25th July 1989 ("Tax Benefits Code").

g) Gratuitous transfers in favour of spouses, parents or remoter forebear, children or remoter issue.

13.8.3. Tax Rates

Stamp duty is levied on the value of each taxable deed or operation at a tax rate, which varies according to the type of deed or operation, as per the examples set out below:

a) Onerous or gratuitous acquisition of immovable assets – 0.8%;

b) Interest paid on the discount of bills of exchange and treasury bills, loans, credit accounts - 4%;

c) Premium and interest on drawn bills, bills receivable, drafts issued in domestic markets or any other kind of transfer - 4%;

d) Commissions in respect of guarantees granted – 3%;

e) Other commissions on financial services rendered - 4%;

f) Incorporation of a company or increase in its share capital by means of issuance of new shares (percentage of the net value of the amount each shareholder is required to pay in order to subscribe to the new company's share capital or the new shares) - 0.4%

g) Transformation of an unincorporated partnership or entity into a company (percentage of the net value of the partnership or entity's assets) – 0.4%;

h) Transfer of a company's place of effective management from an EU Member State or a third country to an EU Member State, if the company's registered office is in a third country (percentage of net value of the company's assets on the date of transfer) – 0,4%.

i)   Onerous transfers of activity - 5%

- Transfer of commercial, industrial or agricultural establishments

 - Sub concession and transfer of concessions provided by state authorities.

j)   Gratuitous transfers – 10%

k)   Acquisitions by *usucapion* -10%

 l) In case of inheritance, stamp duty is levied on the global assets before the partition-10%.

13.9. Tax Benefits

A wide range of tax benefits is granted in various fields of economic, social and cultural activities. Most of them are regulated by the "Tax Benefit Code", as enacted by Decree Law 215/89 of 1st July 1989, as amended, and by the "Code" on each type of tax as well as by separate legislation concerning specific projects or activities. A description of the main areas where tax benefits are available is set out below.

13.9.1. Tax Benefits on Investment Projects

(i)   Investments in production units worth over 4,987,978.97 euros carried out in Portugal until 31st December 2010 and deemed to be relevant for strategic economic sectors, enjoy tax benefits in the form of corporation tax credits and partial or full exemption from "IMI" tax, "IMT" Tax or stamp duty, valid up to 10 years and granted upon the signature of an agreement with the Portuguese Government;

(ii)   Tax incentives for the international expansion of Portuguese companies, namely with regard to investments worth over 249,398.95 euros made by Portuguese companies outside Portugal, are also available in the form of corporation tax credits and elimination of double taxation, where such investment consists of incorporating or acquiring a company abroad, valid up to 5 years, granted upon the signature of an agreement with the Portuguese Government.

 (iii) The extractive and manufacturing industries and the tourist sector are authorized to deduct 20% from the taxable income for 2003 and 2004 financial years in order to create a fiscal reserve to invest in R&D projects or fixed assets. However this tax benefit is not cumulative with any other tax benefit on investment, as per Decree-Law 23/2004 of 23rd January 2004.

13.9.2. Youth Employment

Corporation tax benefits are available in regard to the creation of new jobs for youths under 30, provided that they are employed under an undetermined period employment contract.

13.9.3. Tax Incentives on Research and Technological Development

They are available for the years 2001, 2002 and 2003 and consist of corporation tax credits and tax deductions on certain research and development-related expenses, as per to Decree-Law 292/97of 22nd of October, as amended.

13.9.4. Tax Incentives on Mergers, Demergers, Transfers of Assets and Exchange of Shareholdings

Such operations are covered by a specific corporation tax regime as described in section 13.4.6. above.

13.9.5. Tax Incentives on the Merger or Demerger of State-owned Companies carried out within the Privatisation thereof

Such operations can be exempted from "IMT" tax, stamp duty and notary or registration fees as per Decree-Law 168/90 of 24th May 1990.

13.9.6. Tax Incentives on Capital Markets Activities:

a) Investment Funds: Securities funds and property funds enjoy tax reductions on corporation income and capital gains and, with regard to income arising from investments in such funds, investors are either exempt from individual income tax (private investors) or withholding tax (professional investors);

b) Venture Capital Funds: venture capital funds are exempt from corporation tax. Investors that opt for the aggregation of their income tax can benefit from a 50% deduction on venture capital funds income.

c) Pension Funds, Retirement Funds and Education Funds - These funds are exempt from corporation tax, Tax on the transfer of real estate properties and annual tax on real estate properties and contributions to such funds are partially tax-deductible;

d) Funds constituted by share savings schemes - are exempt from corporation tax and contributions to such schemes are tax deductible up to a certain amount. Share savings schemes are exempt from inheritance tax.

e) Immovable Asset Management and Investment Companies - such companies benefit from a reduced rate of corporation tax (25%) and exemption from Tax on the Transfer of Real Estate Properties and Annual Tax on Real Estate Properties with regard to the acquisition of immovable assets. Such benefits are valid until 2005.

f) Venture Capital Companies and Pure Holding Companies (SGPS) and other companies enjoy the following tax incentives:

(i) Capital gains and losses realised by (SGPS) on the disposal of shareholdings held for at least one year are not included in the calculation of its taxable profits (i.e. gains exempt and losses not deductible);

(ii) In relation to shareholdings acquired from affiliated companies, entities resident in tax heavens or when the company has been transformed into a SGPS, the minimum holding period necessary to exclude the gains from taxation is three years.

g) From January 2003, capital gains arising from the transfer of securities, derivative financial instruments (except swaps) and autonomous warrants are exempt from Individual Income Tax up to 2,500 euros the remainder being taxed on 50% of its value;

h) Capital gains on the transfer of shareholdings held for more than twelve months are exempt from Individual Income Tax

i) Capital gains obtained by non-resident entities on the transfer of shareholdings and other securities are tax-exempt. However, such exemption does not apply to:

(i) Non-resident entities without a permanent establishment in Portugal, if a 25% or higher holding in its share capital is held by a resident entity;

(ii) Persons or entities residing in countries deemed to be "tax havens";

(iii) The transfer of shareholdings in resident companies, if more than 50% of their fixed assets are immovable ones.

(v) The transfer of shareholdings in resident companies that are in a group relationship, as defined by the applicable Credit Institutions and Financial

Companies Regulations, with resident companies that have as fixed assets 50% or more of immoveable assets.

j) Loans granted by non-resident financial entities to resident financial institutions, and swaps between non-resident and resident financial institutions- interest charged on such loans as well as the income arising from the said swaps are exempt from corporation tax. This exemption shall not apply if the interest or income is attributable to a permanent establishment situated in Portugal.

k) Term Bank Accounts held by non-resident financial institutions - interest paid on such accounts is exempt from corporation tax.

l) Income arising from public debt bonds issued in 2002 obtained by non-resident individuals or legal entities - such income is exempt from either Individual or corporation tax.

m) Dividends from shares acquired as a result of the privatisation of a State-owned company in the period up to the end of 2002 - only 50% of the net amount of such dividends is taxed; this benefit is valid for five years from the date the privatisation procedure was completed.

n) The acquisition of shares in the privatisation of a state-owned company until the end of 2002 – up to 5% of the total amount invested on the acquisition, or 7.5 % thereof if the investor is an employee at the privatised undertaking, is individual income tax-deductible.

o) Futures and derivatives contracts operated in the Stock Exchange - income received from these sources by individuals, investment funds or venture capital funds is taxed at a 10% rate. This regime is in place until 31st December 2002.

13.10. Measures Against International Tax Evasion

The Portuguese Tax System contains a number of measures (some were introduced by Law 109-B/2001 of 27th December 2001) intended to curb international tax evasion using schemes involving countries with a "highly favourable tax system" - the so-called "tax havens". These countries are listed in Governmental Order 1272/2001 of 9th November 2001.

13.10.1. Individual Income Tax

13.10.1.1. Transfer of Tax Residence

Resident individuals who transfer their residence to a "tax haven" are considered to be Portuguese residents for taxation purposes in the tax year where the transfer takes place and in the four following tax years, unless they are able to prove that the transfer was due to "justified reasons", namely to carry out a professional activity as employees of a Portuguese-resident company.

13.10.1.2. Tax Deductible Expenses

The following expenses cannot be considered as tax deductible for the purposes of assessing taxable income:

(i)   Amounts paid to entities resident in "tax havens" by way of interest on or redemption of, loans granted for the construction, purchase or improvement of an urban building or a part thereof for residential purposes;

(ii)   Rents paid to individuals or legal entities residing in "tax havens" without a permanent establishment operation in Portugal to which such payments can be attributed, in respect of the lease for residential purposes of an urban building, or part thereof, located within Portugal, except if the annual value of such rents is higher than 1/15 of the taxable value of the building or part thereof.

13.10.1.3. Payments made to Entities residing in "Tax Havens"

The amounts relating to all payments made or due by a resident individual to an entity residing in a "tax haven" are taxed at a 35% tax rate, irrespective of the tax rate applicable to other categories of income, unless the former is able to prove that such payments relate to effective operations and are not "of an abnormal character and exaggerated amount".

13.10.2. Corporation Tax

13.10.2.1. Payments made to Entities residing in "Tax Havens"

Payments made to such entities are not tax deductible, except if the taxpayer proves that they correspond to operations that effectively took place and are not of an abnormal character and exaggerated amount.

13.10.2.2. Attribution to Shareholders of Profits from Companies residing in "Tax Havens"

Profits obtained by a company residing in a "tax haven" are attributed, irrespective of dividend distribution, for corporation tax purposes, to Portuguese-resident corporate shareholders in accordance with their holdings therein, if they are equal to, or higher than, 25% of the said company's share capital, or equal to, or higher than 10% if more than 50% of the said company's share capital is held, directly or indirectly, by Portuguese-resident entities.

This rule does not apply where the company residing in a "tax haven" derives more than 75% of its profits from agricultural, industrial or commercial activities connected with the territory they reside in or are not involved in banking or insurance activities.

The same rules also apply to individual shareholders for individual income tax purposes.

13.10.2.3. Attribution of Property Income to Taxable Profits of Entities residing in "Tax Havens"

Where an entity residing in a "tax haven" owns an urban building located within Portugal, which is neither rented nor used for a determined economic activity, 1/15 of the said building's taxable value shall be attributed by way of property income to the entity's taxable profits for the purposes of corporation tax.

13.10.3. Annual Tax on Real Estate Properties

Annual Tax on Real Estate Properties (IMI) owned by entities residing in a "tax-haven" is collected at a 5% rate, irrespective of whether the said asset is an urban building or construction or rural land.

13.10.4. Tax Benefits

There are certain restrictions on tax benefits, with regard to tax entities residing in "tax havens":

(i)   Temporary IMI exemptions applicable to construction land or urban buildings for sale or resale do not apply if such land or buildings were acquired by an entity residing in a "tax haven";

(ii)   Temporary IMI exemptions with regard to urban buildings or parts thereof constructed or improved for residential purposes do not apply where their proprietor is an entity residing in a "tax haven";

(iii) Temporary IMI exemptions with regard to urban buildings totally or partially leased for residential purposes do not apply where the landlord is an entity residing in a "tax haven";

(iv)   A number of corporation tax exemptions or reductions on financial operations do not apply to entities residing in "tax havens", as described above in section 13.9.6., item h).

13.11. Treaties entered into by Portugal for the Avoidance of Double Taxation

Portugal has signed double tax treaty conventions with a number of countries to avoid the double taxation of income. A chart listing the double tax treaties currently in force as well as the maximum withholding tax rates provided for in each of the treaties is set out below:

CHART TWELVE

COUNTRIES	DATE RATIFIED	RATES		
		DIVIDENDS	INTEREST	ROYALTIES
AUSTRIA	1971	15%	10%	10% c) 5% b)
BELGIUM (1)	1970	15%	15%	10 %
BRAZIL	2001	10%(e) 15%(b)	15%	15%
BULGARIA	1996	10% e) 15% b)	10%	10%
CANADA	2000	10% e) 15% b)	10%	10%
CAPE VERDE	2000	10%	10%	10%
CHINA	2000	10%	10%	10%
CUBA (2)	2001	5% (e) 10% (b)	10%	5%
CZECH REPUBLIC	1997	10% e) 15% b)	10%	10%
DENMARK (3)	2002	10% (i)	10% (j)	10%
FINLAND	1970	10% e) 15% b)	15%	10%
FRANCE	1971	15%	10% f) 12% b)	5%
GERMANY	1982	15%	10% a) 15% b)	10%
GREECE (3)	2002	15%	15%	10%
HUNGARY	1999	10%(e) 15%(b)	10%	10%
ICELAND (3)	2002	10%(e) 15% b)	10%(j)	10%
INDIA	2000	10%(e)	10%	10%

		15%(b)		
IRELAND	1994	15%	15%	10%
ITALY	1982	15%	15%	12%
LITHUANIA	2002	10%	10%	10%
LATVIA	2001	10%	10%	10%
LUXEMBOURG	2000	15%	10%(h) 15%(b)	10%
MACAO	1999	10%	10%	10%
MALTA (3)	2002	10%(e) 15%(b)	10%	10%
MEXICO	2000	10%	10%	10%
MOROCCO	1998	10%(e) 15%(b)	12%	10%
MOZAMBIQUE	1992	15%	10%	10%
NORWAY	1970	10% e) 15% b)	15%	10%
PAKISTAN	2003	10% 15%(i)	10%	10%
POLAND	1997	15%	10%	10%
ROMANIA	1999	10%(e) 15%(b)	10%	10%
RUSSIA (2)	2002	10%(e) 15%(b)	10%	10%
SINGAPORE	2000	10%	10%	10%
SOUTH KOREA	1997	10% e) 15% b)	15%	10%
SPAIN	1995	10% e) 15% b)	15%	5%
SWEDEN	2002	10%	10%	10%
SWITZERLAND	1974	10% e) 15% b)	10%	5%
THE NETHERLANDS	2000	10%	10%	10%

TUNISIA	2000	15%	15%	10%
UKRAINE (3)	2002	10%(e) 15%(b)	10%(j)	10%
UNITED KINGDOM	1968	10% e) 15% b)	10%	5%
UNITED STATES OF AMERICA	1995	10%e) 15%b)	10%	10%
VENEZUELA	1997	10%	10%	12% 10 %(g)

(1)   Amended by an additional Convention ratified by Portugal on 14th December 2000;

(2)   Not yet in force.

(3)   The treaty is already in force but its provisions are only effective from 1st January 2003.

a)   If paid by banking entities;

b)   In all other cases.

c)   Where a company holds 50% or more of the share capital.

d)   Literary, artistic or scientific works, films, etc.

e)   Where a company holds 25% or more of the share capital.

f)   In respect of debentures issued in France after 1st January 1965.

g)   For the supply of technical assistance services.

h)   If paid by companies to financial entities.

i)   No withholding tax shall apply if paid by a company to its subsidiary, provided that the former holds a 25% or higher participation in the latter's share capital for, at least, two consecutive years.

j)   No withholding tax shall apply if paid by, or to, one of the contracting parties, a political subdivision, a municipality, the Central Bank or any public institution.

13.12. Social Security Contributions

Social Security contributions are paid in part by the employer and in part by the employee. The employee's contribution is withheld at source as per the following chart:

CHART THIRTEEN

Regime	Beneficiary	Employer
Employees (dependent work)	11%	23.75%
Members of the management body of a company or any other legal entity (a)	10%	21.25%
Self-employed workers under the minimum (mandatory) protection scheme (b)	25.4%	—
Self-employed workers under the enlarged protection scheme (b)	32%	—

(a)   The amount of the social security contributions may be limited to 12 times the monthly national minimum wage (356.60 Euros x 12 = 4,279.20 euros), where the member concerned receives no remuneration from the company.

(b)   Contributions range between a minimum 356.60 (1 X the monthly national minimum wage) and 4,279.20 euros (12 X the monthly national minimum wage).

UTILITIES:

WATER, ELECTRICITY, NATURAL GAS AND TELECOMMUNICATIONS

CHAPTER 14

14.1. Introduction

The water, electricity, natural gas and telecommunication sectors are essential components of the modern Portuguese economy.

In Portugal, these utilities have always belonged to the state as they have long been regarded as a service of a social, rather than an economic nature. As a consequence, such services were provided either by the state itself or by state-owned firms operating under special or exclusive rights granted by the national authorities.

Nevertheless, in recent years these sectors have been privatised and liberalised as a result of Portugal's integration into the internal market of the European Community.

14.2. European Union Legal Framework

The cornerstone of European Union policy on utilities was the Commission's 1985 White Paper on the completion of the internal market, which contained, *inter alia*, an action programme and a timetable for the opening up of these sectors, from which private firms were previously excluded, including water, natural gas, electricity and telecommunications.

Following the White Paper, the Council adopted Directive 93/38/EEC of 14th June 1993, coordinating the means by which entities operate in the water, energy, transport and telecommunications sectors, which envisaged harmonising Member States' regulations on, and thus stimulating competition in, these areas. This Directive was amended by Council Directive 98/4/EEC of 16th February 1998 and by Commission Directive 2001/78/EC of 13th September 2001.

Directive 98/4/EEC amended the provisions of Directive 93/38/EEC in accordance with the resolutions contained in Council Decision 94/800/EC of 22nd December 1994, concerning the conclusion of the agreements of the Uruguay Round of Multilateral Trade Negotiations (1986-1994), also known as the Final Act. The Uruguay Round approved, *inter alia*, the Agreement on Government Procurement with the purpose of establishing a multilateral framework of balanced rights and obligations with respect to government procurement. This agreement aimed at the liberalisation and expansion of world trade, providing for equal access conditions to government procurement sectors in all the signatory countries to these agreements as well as equality of treatment for all entities operating within the public and the private sector.

The European Parliament is currently discussing a Commission proposal to further amend Directive 93/38/EC, in order to implement the Commission's proposals towards liberalisation of the natural gas and electricity markets, also under discussion at the European Parliament.

Meanwhile, the EU policy on the energy sector also entailed the integration of national energy markets into a common energy market, in order to foster competition between suppliers of energy products, specifically to reduce production costs and ultimately to give energy consumers freedom of choice between suppliers.

The plan adopted by the EU to achieve this objective was developed in a piecemeal fashion.

The first stage consisted of improving the transparency of gas and electricity prices charged to non-household end-users, through the implementation of Council Directive 90/377/EEC of 29th June 1990, and of providing for common regulation of the supply of gas and electricity between the main network grids of the EU, through Council Directive 91/296/EEC of 31st May 1991 on the transit of natural gas through grids and Council Directive 90/547/EEC of 29th October 1990 on the transit of electricity through transmission grids. In addition to these Directives, the European Parliament and the Council adopted Decision no. 1254/96/EC, of 5th June 1996, laying down a series of guidelines for trans-European energy networks.

The second stage, which began in 1992, consisted of eliminating a set of restrictions on equal access for companies in the areas of exploration of hydrocarbons and of the establishment of a common gas and electricity market. These objectives were implemented with the adoption of Directive 96/92/EC of the European Parliament and of the Council of 19th December 1996 concerning common rules for the internal market in electricity and of Directive 98/30/EC of the European Parliament (EP) and of the Council of 22nd June 1998, concerning common rules for the

218

internal market in natural gas. Following a lively debate regarding the nature of third-party access to network grids, the abovementioned Directives allowed for Member States to opt for a single buyer system.

The third and final stage will allow the completion of the internal market. Consequently, the Commission proposed further amendments to Directive 96/92/EC and Directive 98/30/EC, currently under discussion in the European Parliament. According to the Commission's proposal, freedom of choice of electricity and gas suppliers to corporate consumers must be achieved by 2003 and 2004 respectively and freedom of choice of supplier for individual consumers (in both markets) must be reached in 2005. The European Council's Barcelona Summit (March 2002) called for the introduction of freedom of choice as regards supplies of gas and electricity to corporate customers by 2004 and for the adoption by the EP of the amendments to Directives 96/92/EC and 98/30/EC as well as the pending revision of guidelines for trans-European energy networks no later than December 2002.

With regards to the telecommunications sector Commission Directive 90/388/EEC of 28th June 1990, on competition in the markets for telecommunications services, as amended by Commission Directive 96/19/EC of 13th March 1996, and by Commission Directive 99/64/EC of 23rd June 1999, recently revoked by Commission Directive 2002/77/EC of 16th September 2002, was the cornerstone in the development of telecommunications services, as it opened such markets to competition. Two more landmarks are Directive 97/33/EC of the European Parliament and of the Council of 30th June 1997, on interconnection in Telecommunications with regard to ensuring universal service and interoperability through application of the principles of Open Network Provision (ONP) and Directive 98/10/EC of the European Council and of the European Parliament of 26th February 1998 on the application of the Open Network Provision (ONP) to vocal telephony on universal service telecommunications in an open and competitive environment.

The European Parliament and the Council adopted in 7th March 2002 the so-called "telecommunications package", comprised of:
- Directive 2002/21/EC of the European Parliament and of the Council on a common regulatory framework for electronic communications networks and services (Framework Directive);
- Directive 2002/19/EC of the European Parliament and of the Council on access to, and interconnection of, electronic communications networks and associated facilities (Access Directive);

- Directive 2002/20/EC of the European Parliament and of the Council on the authorisation of electronic communications networks and services (Authorisation Directive);

- Directive 2002/22/EC of the European Parliament and of the Council on universal service and users' rights relating to electronic communications networks and services (Universal Service Directive);

- Decision 676/2002/EC of the European Parliament and of the Council on a regulatory framework for radio spectrum policy in the European Community (Radio Spectrum Decision).

These Directives and this Decision to replace the Directives referred to above constitute a comprehensive reform of the regulatory framework for the telecommunications market. They envisage the simplification of the said framework and ensure consistency of national regulations across the EU, by, *inter alia*, giving the Commission powers to require national regulatory authorities to amend or withdraw a draft measure if the Commission considers that this measure may create a barrier to the single European market or infringe Community law.

In January 2002, Member States have been given a 15-month period to implement the "Telecommunications package".

Still in 2002, The European Parliament and the Council adopted Directive 2002/58/EC of 12th July 2002 on privacy and electronic communications.

14.3. Water

14.3.1. Portuguese Legal Framework

The legal framework concerning water resources is composed of a vast amount of legislation, the most important of which are the following:

a)   Law no. 88-A/97 of 25th July 1997, laying down the legal framework on access of private entities to basic economic sectors;

b) Decree-Law 46/94 of 22nd February 1994, as amended by Decree-Law 234/98 of 22nd July 1998 regulating access to water resources in general.

c) Decree-Law 379/93, as amended by Law 176/99 of 25th October 1999 and Decree-Law 439-A/99 of 29th October 1999, by Decree-Law 319/94 of 24th December 1994 and by

Decree-Law 14/2002 of 26th January 2002 regulating municipal and multi-municipal systems for water extraction, treatment and distribution for public consumption as well as treatment and discharge of urban wastewater, and treatment and disposal of urban solid waste.

d) Decree-Law 236/98, of 1st August 1998, as amended by Decrees-Law 52/99, 53/99 and 54/99 of 20th February 1999 and by Decree-Law 243/2001 of 5th September 2001, setting out quality standards for water for human consumption as well as quality control mechanisms and incorporating provisions of the Council Directive 80/778/EC of 15th July 1980 and the principles contained in the then draft Council Directive relating to the quality of water for human consumption, later adopted as Directive 98/83/EC of 3rd November 1998.

e) Decree-Law 152/97, of 19th June 1997, as amended by Decree-Law 261/99 of 7th July 1999, incorporating Directive 91/271/EEC of 21st May 1991 and Directive 98/15/EC of 21st February 1998, both relating to urban wastewater treatment and to Wastewater Treatment Plants *(Estações de Tratamento de Águas Residuais - ETAR)* as amended by Decree-Law 172/2001 of 26th of May 2001; and

f) Government Order *(Portaria)* 992/95 of 17th August 1995, regulating prices for the sale of water for human consumption as well as for the rental of water meters.

14.3.2. Access to Water Resources in General

In most cases, third party access to water resources requires prior governmental authorisation. These areas include:

i)   Water extraction;

ii)   Discharge of wastewater;

iii)   Hydraulic infrastructure and other constructions located near water resources.

Such authorisation is granted either through a 10 or 35-year maximum duration licence, depending on the purpose of the licence, or under a public concession agreement, valid up to 75 years.

Prior licensing is required for such activities as water extraction for self-consumption and production of hydroelectric energy in facilities which generate power under 10 Megawatts (*mini-hídricas* or Mini-dams).

A public concession agreement is required for such activities as water extraction for human consumption, if intended for public distribution and production of hydroelectric energy in facilities, which generate power of more than 10 Megawatts.

The above mentioned licences are awarded by the *Direcções Regionais do Ambiente e do Planeamento do Território* (DRAOT - the Regional Offices of the Environment Ministry) while the public concession agreements must be approved by the Environment Minister.

Operation under licenses or concession agreements is overseen by the DRAOT and by the National Water Institute (*Instituto Nacional da Água* - INAG), which is the administrative body in charge of managing water resources in Portugal.

14.3.3. Access to Water Extraction, Treatment and Distribution for Public Consumption

Water extraction, treatment and distribution for public consumption as well as urban wastewater treatment, discharge, urban solid waste treatment and disposal can be carried out through multi-municipal or municipal systems. Multi-municipal systems ensure water supply to, or treatment and disposal of urban wastewater and solid waste within, an area that covers the territory of two or more municipalities, while the municipal systems relate to water distribution and wastewater/solid waste treatment and disposal within the territory of a single municipality.

Since such utilities are publicly owned, as per Law 88-A/97 of 25th July 1997, mentioned in item 14.3.1. above, management of multi-municipal and municipal systems is only possible through public concession agreements.

14.3.3.1. Multi-municipal Systems

Public concession agreements on multi-municipal systems are awarded by the Government via Decree-Law to a company jointly owned by the state or municipalities and private investors who cannot be majority shareholders.

The concession agreements must establish all the business conditions, such as (i) the purpose of the concession, which includes the construction and/or acquisition of all facilities and equipment necessary to operate the concession, (ii) dates, (iii) technical expertise, (iv) capital investment, (v) tariffs charged by concession holder, (vi) the facility construction schedule, among others.

The duration of the concession can vary between 10 and 50 years.
Upon termination of the concession agreement, all the assets relating to the concession will become state property.

14.3.3.2. Municipal Systems

The management of a municipal system is awarded by the respective municipality to a company wholly or partially owned by private investors, through a public concession agreement by means of a public tendering process.

The concession agreement is valid for a period of 10 to 50 years and its remit includes the construction and/or acquisition of all facilities and equipment to carry out the concession.

Under the concession agreement the concession holder has an exclusive right to pursue the activities foreseen therein and the pursuit of such activities by another party is therefore illegal.

Upon the expiry of the concession agreement all the assets relating to the concession will become municipal property.

14.3.3.3. Supervision

Concession holders within any of the abovementioned systems are regulated by several entities, such as the Public Health Department (*Direcção Geral de Saúde*), which oversees sanitation, the Environment Department (*Direcção Geral do Ambiente*), which is the entity responsible for the treatment and collection of the information in order to ensure compliance with legal rules and the Environment General Inspection Department (*Inspecção Geral do Ambiente*), which carries out inspection programmes.

14.4. Electricity

14.4.1. Portuguese Legal Framework

14.4.1.1. Ending the State Monopoly on the Electricity Market

(i) Electricity production, transportation and distribution was until the late 1980's publicly owned via *EDP – Electricidade de Portugal, EP*.

(ii) However, in 1991, the government converted EDP, until then a state-owned enterprise, into a public company whose share capital was 100% owned by the state. In 1997 and 1998, the government opened EDP to private ownership by selling 49,2 % of its holding in EDP's share capital. In 2000, it disposed of another 20%, leaving the state with 30,8% of EDP's share capital as of this date.

14.4.1.2. Opening Up the Electricity Market to Private Operators

(i)   Until 1988, private entities could only undertake small-scale hydroelectric energy production (under 1 Megawatt) and electricity generation based on renewable resources and the combined production of thermal and electric power (co-generation), currently regulated by Decree-Law 189/88 of 27th May 1988, as amended by Decrees-Law 168/99 of 18th May 1999 and 339-C/2001 of 29th December.

(ii)   The first step towards the liberalisation of the sector was the approval of Decree-Law 449/88 of 10th December 1988, amending Law 46/77 of 8th July 1977 (later revoked by Law no. 88-A/97 of 25th July 1997), which fully opened the electricity generation sector to private entities.

(iii)   The second step was taken with Decree-Laws 182/95 to 188/95, of 27th July 1995, which regulated in detail the structure and features of the electricity sector, covering separately the generation, distribution and transmission of electricity, and also creating an electricity supervisory entity and an electricity generation planning authority.

(iv) These Decree-Laws were later amended by Decree-Laws 56/97 of 14th March and 198/2000 of 24th August - which also revoked Decree-Law 188/95 - in order to implement Directive no. 96/92/EC of 19th December 1996 on the common market for electricity and further increase the liberalisation of the electricity sector, namely as regards electricity transmission. The said amendments were also a result of the privatisation of EDP.

14.4.2. The National Electricity Generation, Transmission and Distribution System (*Sistema Eléctrico Nacional - SEN*)

The SEN consists of the following two subsystems:

a)   The Public Electricity System (*Sistema de Electricidade de Serviço Público* - SEP);

b)   The Independent Electricity System (*Sistema Eléctrico Independente* - SEI).

14.4.2.1. The Public Electricity System (SEP - *Sistema Eléctrico de Serviço Público*)

The SEP's purpose is to generate, distribute and transmit electricity to the whole country on a public service basis (which means competition is not allowed within the SEP). It is composed of:

- The National Grid Operator (*Rede Nacional de Transporte de Energia Eléctrica - RNT*), which holds the monopoly of electricity transmission within Portugal;

- Electricity generators and distributors engage with the SEP in power purchase or distribution agreements.

225

14.4.2.1.1. Electricity Generation and Distribution within the SEP

Electricity generation within the SEP is based on long-term Power Purchase Agreements (PPAs) concluded between the National Grid Operator (RNT) and each electricity generator, under which the latter is obliged to supply the SEP exclusively with all the electricity generated. The return on the PPAs is based on two tariffs: (i) the Capacity Charge, based on the production capacity set out in the PPA and whose purpose it is to provide a return on the fixed costs incurred by producers, with all operational cost savings reverting towards the gennerator, and (ii) the Energy Charge, whose purpose is to stimulate the efficient use of resources and seeks to give a return on variable costs incurred (mostly fuel used in the production of electricity), i.e., the costs incurred in the actual production of electricity as calculated in relation to current market prices, whereby the savings, if any, revert to the producer.

High-, medium- and low-voltage electricity distributors within the SEP are required to engage in Power Distribution Agreements (PDA) with the RNT, under which they undertake to acquire only the electricity produced by the RNT or by PPA-bound electricity producers and distribute it only to SEP operators. Tariffs to be charged are set out in the tariff regulation as approved by the Electrical Supervisory Authority.

Decree-Law 182/95 of 27th July 1995 as amended by Decrees-Law 56/97 of 14th March 1997 and 24/99 of 28th January 1999 granted licences to PDA - distributors for the North, Centre, Lisbon & Tejo Valley, South distribution areas. These distributors are four "EDP, SA" subsidiaries resulting from "EDP"'s restructuring upon its conversion into a public company in 1990 and were later merged into "EDP-Distribuição Energia, SA", an "EDP, SA" subsidiary whose sole object is electricity distribution. The purpose of this merger was to separate electricity production from electricity distribution fully, as a measure to improve market openness and transparency, in compliance with Directive no. 96/92/EC;

14.4.2.2. The Independent Electricity System (*Sistema Eléctrico Independente* - SEI)

The SEI is managed on a commercial basis and allows competition between operators. It is composed of:

a) The Independent Electricity Production and Distribution System (*Sistema Eléctrico não-Vinculado* - SENV) in which High and Medium voltage electricity producers and distributors can pursue their respective activities either for their own consumption or for commercial purposes;

b) Electricity production from hydroelectric facilities, which generate a maximum 10 Megawatts;

c) Electricity production based on other renewable resources;

d) Electricity production by means of combined heat and electricity production (co-generation) facilities;

e) Low-voltage electricity production based on micro-generators (i.e., up to 150 Kilowatts) for the producer's own consumption.

14.4.2.2.1. Electricity Generation and Distribution within the SEI

Access to the SEI is free, that is, any private entity can become a SENV electricity generator or distributor. SEI operators are free to choose their clients and are therefore not required to generate or distribute electricity for or from SEP operators alone. SEI operators are also free to establish the terms of the agreements concluded with their clients.

14.4.2.3. Transmission of Electricity

Transmission of electricity is carried out exclusively by the National Grid Operator (*Rede Nacional de Transporte de Energia Eléctrica* - RNT), which has been kept in public ownership. Thus, the RNT must be managed under a concession agreement on a public service basis. The majority of the concession holder' share capital must be owned by the state, either directly or indirectly, the current concession holder being "EDP - Distribuição Energia, SA", an "EDP, SA" subsidiary. The RNT concession holder is obliged to ensure that SEP distributors are duly supplied with electricity in accordance with the respective Power Distribution Agreements and to grant SENV operators access to the National Grid Network wherever required by their respective activities.

14.4.3. Regulatory Authority

The electricity production, distribution and transmission sector is supervised by the Energy Regulatory Authority (*Entidade Reguladora dos Serviços Energéticos* -), which is a legal entity governed by Public Law which has been granted with financial and administrative independence. The Energy Regulatory Authority oversees the Public Electricity System (SEP) and the commercial relationship between SEP and SEI operators and is empowered to impose the tariff regulation applicable to SEP operators. The Energy Regulatory Authority also has an arbitration function with regard to disputes arising from the trade or contractual relationship between the National Grid Operator, electricity producers or distributors and electricity consumers.

14.4.4 Energy Administration

The general managing body for Energy (*Direcção-Geral da Energia* - DGE) is the government body responsible for the administration of energy. It has the following duties: i) To carry out the studies necessary to assist the Government in making decisions on energy policy; ii) To propose legislation to regulate the sector and to supervise compliance with the legislation in force; iii) To grant licenses to electricity production and/or distribution facilities and equipment, to establish the technical regulations and specifications that such facilities and equipment must comply with; iv) To issue approvals for energy-related products, processes and systems and certify the competent bodies which may intervene in the energy sector; v) To manage programmes designed to support initiatives which are part of the energy policy outlined by the Government; vi) To encourage the spread of information to energy users/consumers, particularly the provision of statistical information on the sector and information on national energy policy issues.

14.5. Natural Gas

14.5.1. Portuguese Legal Framework

Decree-Law 374/89, of 25th October 1989, as amended by Decree-Law 232/90, of 16th July, by Decree-Law 274-A/93 of 4th August, by Decree-Law 8/2000 of 8th February, first regulated the importation, storage, treatment, transportation and distribution of natural gas and laid down the principles governing the natural gas public concession service in Portugal.

Decree-Law 14/2001, of 27th January, which incorporated Directive 98/30/EC, laid down the principles that govern the Portuguese natural gas market as well as the duties of natural gas market operators.

The Council of Minister's Resolution no. 150/98 of 23rd December 1998 called for the construction of a natural gas reception and storage station within Portugal. This Council of Minister's Resolution justified this measure because of the necessity of liberalising the Portuguese natural gas market in view of its integration into the single market and for the economic benefits of having a range of energy sources in order to reduce dependence on oil products given the effects of high crude oil prices in international markets.

Natural gas distribution and transportation must also abide by the following regulations:

a)   Decree-Law 262/89 of 17th July 1989 as amended by Decrees-Law 219/91 of 17th June, which regulates the installation of gas transmission grids and 178/92 of 14th August;

b)   Decree-Law 263/89 of 17th July 1989, as amended by Decree-Law 232/90 of 16th July 1990, approving the procedures for certification of gas transmission grid installation and maintenance technicians and/or firms;

c)   Decree-Law 232/90 of 16th July 1990, as amended by Decree-Law 183/94 of 1st July 1994 and Decree-Law 7/2000 of 3rd February, which sets out the principles relating to the planning, construction, exploitation and maintenance of gas transmission and supply systems;

d)   Decree-Law 521/99, of 10th December 1999, relating to gas installations in buildings as well as their maintenance.

14.5.2. Access to the Activities of Importation, Transmission and Distribution of Natural Gas

Importation and transmission of natural gas consists of acquiring, receiving, storing and treating natural gas as well as of its transport through high-pressure pipelines and supply to distributors or consumers. Distribution of natural gas comprises the reception, storage, and treatment of natural gas as well as supplying low-pressure natural gas via regional or local distribution pipelines or local supply depots. These activities must be pursued either under a public concession agreement (where they are considered a public service) or under license.

14.5.2.1.   Natural Gas Importation, Transportation and Distribution Under Public Concession Agreements - the following activities can only be pursued under a public concession agreement:

(i) Natural gas importation, transportation and supply through high-pressure pipelines;

(ii) The distribution and supply of natural gas through low-pressure regional pipelines.

The concession agreements must be approved by the Council of Ministers. Concessions for natural gas importation and distribution through high-pressure pipelines are awarded through a private treaty procedure while the concessions for the distribution and supply of natural gas through low-pressure regional pipelines are awarded through tendering procedures. The activities comprised within the concession agreement are exercised in an exclusive manner. The concession agreements are valid for a maximum 40 years.

14.5.2.2. Natural Gas Distribution and Supply Under License. A license is required for operating in the following areas:

(i)   Management of local natural gas pipelines installed in areas not covered by regional pipelines;

(ii)   Management of local supply depots;

(iii)   Private natural distribution, i.e. natural gas distribution for self-consumption or to third parties in areas not covered by either a regional or local pipeline.

As a rule, licensed entities conduct their respective activities on a competitive, market-oriented basis; they are not required to fulfil public service obligations, like concession agreement holders do, except for licensees for the management of local natural gas transmission grids, who are required to operate on a public service basis, their rights and obligations being identical to those of concession agreement holders These licenses are awarded by the Minister for the Economy and are valid for a maximum of 20 years (management of local grids) or 10 years (management of local supply depots).

14.5.2.3.Natural Gas Importation, Transportation and Distribution Under Decree-Law 14/2001 of 27th January

Decree-Law 14/2001 further developed the system referred to above, in compliance with Directive 98/30/EC by creating several additional obligations to be fulfilled by concession or license holders:

a)   The duty to operate, maintain and develop an economically viable, secure, efficient and reliable natural gas transmission, storage or distribution system;

b)   A duty of confidentiality as regards all commercial information obtained through other operators or third parties as well as a duty to disclose non-commercial information relevant for safe and efficient management of interconnected pipeline networks;

c)   A duty to keep separate accounts for their natural gas transmission, distribution and storage activities, and, where appropriate, consolidated accounts for non-gas activities. The said Decree-Law also laid down the means by which customers may be attracted to new gas suppliers, as defined in article 15 of Directive 98/30/EC, in accordance with an additional regulation to be adopted no later than 2007 (i.e., upon the expiration of the derogations allowed by Directive 98/30/EC to emergent (less than 10 years old) markets like the Portuguese one).

14.6. Telecommunications

The telecommunications sector covers the areas of telegraph, telephone, telex and data communication services, as well as videophone, facsimile, teletext and videotext.

14.6.1. Portuguese Legal Framework

The key legal regulations on the telecommunications services sector are the following:
i) Decree- Law 31/2003 of 17th February and Law 91/97 of 1st August 1997, as amended by Law 29/2002 of 6th December, (Basic Telecommunications Law) - laid down the basic principles governing the establishment, management and exploitation of telecommunications networks and the provisions of telecommunications services.

(ii) Decree-Law 458/99 of 5th November 1999, which developed the regulations on the universal telecommunications service enshrined in Law 91/97.

(iii) Decree-Law 381-A/97 of 30th December 1997, as amended by Decree-Law 92/99 of 23rd March 1999, regulates access to operation of public telecommunications networks and provision of public telecommunications services by private companies;

(iv) Decree-Law 290-A/99 of 30th July 1999, as amended by Decree-Law 249/2001 of 21st September 2001, which sets out the general conditions for the operation of public telecommunications networks in Portugal;

(v) Decree-Law 241/97 of 18th September 1997 as amended by Decree-Law 192/2000 of 18th August 2000, regulates the operation of cable television networks;

(vi) Decree-Law 309/2001 of 7th December 2001 instating the Portuguese Communications Regulatory Authority (*Autoridade Nacional de Comunicações – ANACOM*.

14.6.2. Access to Telecommunications Services Provision Activities

Telecommunications services include the activity of transmission, reception or broadcast of signals, representation of symbols, writing, pictures sounds or information of any nature by means of wires, optic systems, radio signals and other electromagnetic systems.

Law 91/97 classifies telecommunications and telecommunications services as public utilities if they are intended for the general public, or as private utilities, if they are intended for personal use or for a limited numbers of users. Accordingly, telecommunication networks (i.e., the physical/ electromagnetic means of signal broadcasting, transmission, or reception) are classified as public utilities where they fully or partially serve public telecommunications services and private utilities where they serve private telecommunications services.

14.6.2.1. Provision of the Universal Telecommunications Service

In line with the directives referred to in item 14.6.1. above, Law 91/97 enshrined the principle of liberalisation of telecommunications and ensured the availability of a universal telecommunications service, defined as the duties inherent to the provision of public telecommunications services, in a continuous and equitable manner, all over the country, in order to fulfil the communication necessities of the Portuguese people. The universal service is comprised of a fixed telephone service (which may include the provision of switched access services for data transmission and leased circuit services and can be provided by the state, public corporate bodies or by private entities through concession agreements.

The regulations on universal service were developed by Decree-Law 458/99 of 5th November 1999, which also set out the universal service pricing and financing systems, and takes into consideration the principles of universality, equality, continuity and affordability.

The same Decree-Law also designated "Portugal Telecom, S.A." (PT) as the Universal Service Provider.

PT, the largest company in Portugal, still holds a dominant position in the provision of fixed telephony services, even though this sector was fully liberalised on 1st January 2001, and it is expected to continue to do so in the medium term. For this reason, PT has certain obligations towards other operators, specifically: i) it holds a concession for the management of the national telecommunication substructures; ii) it is required by Law to render interconnection services to the new operators, since these do not yet have their own interconnection substructures and therefore depend on PT's interconnection services.

14.6.2.2 Operation of Public Telecommunications Networks and Provision of Public Telecommunications Services

A license and/or registration is required to become a Public Telecommunications Network Operator and Public Use Telecommunications Service Provider. Such licenses are awarded by the Portuguese Communications Regulatory Authority (*Autoridade Nacional de Comunicações - ANACOM*). Where the said activities entail the allocation of a radio frequency through a tendering procedure, the respective license is granted by the member of the Government responsible for the communications area.

As a rule, the provision of telecommunications services is subject to mere registration with ANACOM. However, a license is required:

i)   For the provision of fixed telephone services;

ii)   For the establishment and/or provision of public telecommunications networks;

iii)   For the granting of frequencies for the establishment of networks or the provision of services;

iv)   For the fulfilment of duties to provide universal telecommunications services, open network or interconnection services which flow from holding a significant position in the market.

With Decree-Law 92/99 of 23rd March 1999 the existing protection in the sector was revoked since it was considered that the dynamism of this area and its progress no longer justified such "protection", in line with the liberalisation trend set out by Directive 96/19/EC.

14.6.2.3. Public Telecommunication Networks

Decree-Law 290-A/99, of 30th July 1999, referred to above, lays out the general conditions regulating the operation of public telecommunications networks in Portugal, including the rights and duties of public telecommunications operators, with the purpose of ensuring the provision of an open network and of leased circuit services.

Decree-Law 241/97 of 18th September 1997 as amended by Decree-Law 192/2000 of 18th August 2000, covers cable television networks, including the installation and operation of transmission and retransmission facilities, in particular, the distribution of radio and television programmes produced by the operator itself and/or by third parties, whether encoded or not, and the supply of transmission services to third parties.

14.6.2.4. Private Telecommunication Networks

Private Telecommunication Networks are those, which exclusively support services provided for personal use or for a restricted number of users. All individuals or legal entities may install and manage private networks as a communication support for their own use or for a restricted number of persons, provided that such installation/management is undertaken for non-commercial purposes or where no remuneration is involved.

14.6.2.5. Provision of Public Telecommunications Services

The provision of public telecommunications services is regulated by Decree-Law 290-B/99 of 30th July 1999 and consists of:

i) Mobile telecommunications services;

ii) Mobile communication services operated via satellite;

iii) Satellite mobile telecommunications services;

iv) Fixed telecommunications services.

The Decree-Law does not apply to the provision of broadcasting telecommunication services.

These services are supplied by public telecommunications services providers registered or licensed in accordance with Decree-Law 381-A/97 of 30th December.

14.6.3. Telecommunication Supervisory Entities

i) State

The state is obliged to define strategic guidelines and general policies, to approve the applicable legislation for the sector, and to supervise and inspect telecommunications activities and telecommunications operators. The state is also responsible for the management and surveillance of the "public radio-electric domain" (the space through which radio-electric waves can be disseminated).

ii) Portuguese Communications Regulatory Authority (*Autoridade Nacional de Comunicações - ANACOM*).

Formerly known as *Instituto de Comunicações de Portugal* (ICP), ANACOM is the regulatory authority for the telecommunications sector. It assists the Government in relation to telecommunications policy and legislation and, *inter alia*, is empowered to:

i)   Manage the radio-electric spectrum, including the planning, surveillance and allocation of spectral resources;

ii)   Certify telecommunications equipment as well to set technical standards within the telecommunications sector; and

iii)   Enforce the legal and administrative provisions for telecommunications, and subsequently apply any corresponding sanctions.

14.6.4. Market Tendencies: UMTS and DVB

UMTS - Universal Mobile Telecommunications System represents the next step in European telecommunications market.

UMTS is the European version of the global family of technical standards for third generation mobile communications: IMT 2000 – International Mobile Telecommunications. With considerable technological advances it is the successor for the second generation (GSM and DCS) and first generation (mobile analogue communications) systems.

UMTS, whose data transmission can be as high as 2 Megabytes, will enable the supply of multimedia services, with capacity for video transmission through portable terminals and opens the door to convergence with other technologies with transmission capability.

Four UMTS operation licenses were awarded by ANACOM through a public tender on 19th December 2000. UMTS operation under these licenses was supposed to begin 1st January 2002, however, on the licensees' request and due to the technical difficulties in implementing the new system, the Government postponed the introduction of UMTS operation until 31st December 2002.

DVB-T (*Digital Video Broadcasting for Terrestrial Television*) is expected to be the next giant step in this sector, since it enables the supply of multimedia services via television. ANACOM awarded, through a public tender, a DVB-T operation license to "PTDP - Plataforma de Televisão Digital Portuguesa, S.A". Under this license DVB-T operation is to begin no later than 31st August 2002.

BIBLIOGRAPHIC REFERENCES

- The Shipping Register of Madeira: questionnaire.

- The Shipping Register of Madeira

www.sdm.pt

- The International Maritime Organization

www.imo.org

- Financial Privacy Consultants: The Privacy News Letter

http://www1.privacy-consultants.com/nlet/privacy_battle/nlet_05_1997.shtml

- Shipping and Yacht Registration

http://www.consumoffshore.com/english/offind/ship-yacht.html

- The Island of Madeira

http://www.consumoffshore.com/english/countries/madeira.html

- Tax Time E-Trade Management, Lda.

http://www.ttt-madeira.com/MAR/yacht_registration1.html

- *"Ship Management and Maritime Operations"*, New Madeira Investment Serviços, Lda.

http://www.lowtax.net/lowtax/html/jmdobs.html#ship

- *"International Shipping Register – MAR"*

http://offshoregate.com/Portugal.htm

- *"Madeira: Global Solutions for Wise Investments"*, International Business Centre of Madeira, September 2003

www.ibc-madeira.com

- "O novo regime Fiscal das SGPS ", by GUERREIRO Tiago Caiado, Vida Económica, Porto, November 2003.

- "O Sistema Fiscal Português " by Associação Industrial Portuguesa Câmara de Comércio e Indústria, September 2003.

- "Orçamento de Estado para 2004" by Câmara dos Técnicos Oficiais de Contas, Lisboa, February 2004.

- "Imposto sobre o Valor Acrescentado" by LIMA, Emanuel Vidal, Porto Editora, January 2003.

- "Imposto sobre o Rendimento das Pessoas Colectivas" by FERREIRA, Lurdes, Lidel, December 2001.

- "Guia dos Impostos em Portugal" by CARLOS, Américo Brás, ABREU, Irene Antunes, DURÃO, João Ribeiro, PIMENTA, Maria Emília, Quid Juris, Lisboa,2003.

237

- "Impostos sobre o Património " by Dislivro, Lisbon, January 2004

- "Direcção Geral de Contribuições e Impostos"

http: //www.dgci.min-financas.pt/dgciappl/codigosdgci/

- *"The New Portuguese Taxation Regime for Mergers, Demergers, Transfers of Assets and Exchange of Shares"*, by CAMEIRA, Maria Antónia, London, in the International Company and Commercial Law Review (ICCLR), London, England, March 2002.

- *"Direito das Obrigações"*, by COSTA, Mário Júlio de Almeida Costa, 9ª edição, October 2001, Almedina

- *"Contratos Comerciais – Legislação, Doutrina e Jurisprudência"*, by NETO, Abílio, 1ª edição, May 2002, Ediforum, Edições Júridicas, Lda

- *"Noções Fundamentais de Direito Civil"*, by COSTA, Mário Júlio de Almeida Costa, 4ª edição, October 2001, Almedina

- *"Direito Societário Português – Algumas Questões"*, by LABAREDA, João, 1998, Quid Juris?

- *"Sociedades Gestoras de Participações Sociais – Aspectos Jurídicos, Fiscais e Contabilísticos"*, by BORGES, António and MACEDO, João Carlos Monteiro de, 3ª edição, 2002, Àreas Editora

- Report of High level Group of Company Law Experts on a Modern Regulatory framework for company law in Europe (Winter Report), Brussels, 4th November 2002.

- *" ICGN Comments on the 3rd Winter Report - A Modern Regulatory Framework for Company Law in Europe"*, by GOOBEY, Alastair Ross,

http://www.icgn.org/documents/CommentsWinterIIIfair.pdf

- *"The Modern Corporation and Private Property"*, by BEARLE A. and G. MEANS, 1932, NY, World Inc.

- *"Report of the High Level Group of Company Law Experts on a Modern Regulatory Framework for Company Law in Europe"*, WINTER, Jaap (chairman), November 2002

 http://www.ecgi.org/publications/documents/report_en.pdf

- *"Código das Sociedades Comerciais – Jurisprudência e Doutrina"*, by NETO, Abílio, 2º edição, March 2003, Ediforum, Edições Júridicas, Lda

- *"Alterações do Contrato de Sociedade"*, by VENTURA, Raúl, 2ª edição, 1996, Almedina

- *"Novos Estudos Sobre Sociedades Anónimas e Sociedades em Nome Colectivo"*, by VENTURA, Raúl, 1994, Almedina

- *"Sociedades por Quotas"*, by VENTURA, Raúl, 1999, Almedina

- *"Audit Committees Combined Code Guidance (Smith Report)"*, by SMITH, Robert, January 2003

www.ecgi.com

- Share Ownership, Takeover Law and the Contestability of Corporate Control, by FERRARINI, Guido, Centre for Law and Finance, 2001, presented in the Conference *"Company Law Reform in OECD Countries. A Comparative Outlook of Current Trends"*, held in Stockholm on 7-8 December 2000.

-*"Direito dos Valores Mobiliários"*, by Instituto dos Valores Mobiliários, 1999, Coimbra Editora

- *"Special Study on Market Structure, Listing Standards and Corporate Governance"*, American Bar Association (ABA), 17th May 2002.

- *"Takeover Bids and Target Director's Incentives: The Impact of a Bid on Director's Wealth and Board Seats"*, by HARFORD, Jarrad, School of Business Administration, University of Washington, Seattle.

- *"An American Perspective on the New German Anti-takeover Law"*, by GORDON, Jeffrey, June 2002, Columbia Law School, The Center for Law and Economic Studies, in http://ssrn.com/abstract_id=336420

- *"A OPA Obrigatória"*, by MENEZES, FALCÃO, João, in Direito dos Valores Mobiliários, III, Instituto dos Valores Mobiliários, Coimbra Editora, 2001, pages 179-227.

- *"A informação no Mercado dos Valores Mobiliários"*, by PAZ FERREIRA, Eduardo, in Direito dos Valores Mobiliários, III, Instituto dos Valores Mobiliários, Coimbra Editora, 2001, pages 137-178.

- *"Overcoming Mounting Anglo-American Shareholders Concerns"*, by MONKS, Robert and SYKES, Allen, www.ragm.com/library/topics/ragm_sykes.html

- *"Regulatory Framework of Management Buyout Operations in Portugal"*, by CAMEIRA, Maria Antónia and ALBUQUERQUE, Luis, London, England, in International Company and Commercial Law Review (ICCLR), London, England, April 2002.

- Work paper concerning the listed companies legal duty to disclose relevant information to the CMVM, by CMVM www.cmvm.pt

- *"Board-level employee representation in Europe"*, in European Industrial Relations Observatory. http://www.eiro.eurofound.ie/1998/09/study/TN9809201S.html

- *"Board Independence and Long Term Firm Performance"*, by BHAGAT, Sanjai and BLACK, Bernard, February 2000. http://www.law.columbia.edu/lawec/

- *"Break-Trough in European Takeover Regulation?"*, by BERGLÖF, Erik and BURKART, Mike, prepared for the 36th Panel Meeting of Economic Policy in Copenhagen, September 2002.

- *"Capitalism without owners will fail – A policymakers Guide to Reform"*, by MONKS, Robert and SYKES, Allen

www.ragm.com/library/topics/ragm_sykesPolicyMakersGuide.html

- *"Comparative Study of Corporate Governance Codes Relevant to the European Union and its Member States, on behalf of the European Commission, Internal Market Directorate General, Final Report & Annexes I-III"*, undertaken by Weil, Gotshal & Manges LLP, in consultation with EASD and ECGN, and contributors, January 2002.

- *"Corporate Governance in OECD Member Countries: recent developments and trends"*, by OECD steering group on Corporate Governance, April 2001.

- *"Corporate Governance and Responsibility. Foundations of Market Integrity"*, by WITHERELL, Bill, Head OECD Director for Financial, Fiscal and Entreprise Affairs, in Observer n.234, October 2002.

- *"Corporate Governance in Europe"*, by American Enterprise Institute for Public Policy Research Statement of the European shadow Financial Regulatory Committee, London, December 2002.

- *"Corporate Governance and Merger Activity in the U.S.: Making sense of the 1980's and 1990's"*, by HOLENSTROM Bengt and KAPLAN, Steven, February 15, 2001.

- *"Corporate Governance and the Role of Non-Executive directors: an Interim Solution for Insurance Company Boards"*, by Deloitte & Touche.

www.deloitte.co.uk

- *"Corporate Governance: Effects on Firm Performance and Economic Growth"*, by MAHER, Maria and ANDERSSON, Thomas, Organisation for Economic Co-operation and Development, February 2000.

- *"Defensive Measures Adopted by the Board: Current European Trends"*, by CÂMARA, Paulo, presented in the Conference on "Company Law Reform in OECD Countries. A comparative outlook of current trends", held in Stockholm on 7-8 December 2000.

- *"DTI Consultative Document on Director's Remuneration, Corporate Progress Report Update"*, by Deloitte & Touche

www.deloitte.com

- European Business Forum: articles

www.ebf.com

- Corporate Governance ...Lisbon stirs the debate, speeches by NUNES, João Belchior, CADBURY, Adrian and BORGES, António.

- *"Board Performance Not Just Board Conformance"*, by GARRAT, Bob.

- *"Why the days of "non-execs" may be numbered"*, by COORSH, Jeffrey.

- *"Is Corporate Governance Delivering Value?"*
- *"Corporate Governance: First Principles, Current Debates and Future Prospects"*, by LAZZARI, Valter.
- *"Corporate Governance and Value: Appearance and Reality"*, by MONKS, Robert.
- *"Why Standards may be Converging"*, by CADBURY, Adrian.
- *"Accountability and State Companies"*, by DEMALTTÈ, Claudio.
- *"Beyond Corporate Governance: from local to global"*, by Van den BERGHE, Lutgart.
- *"Three ideas for the "two-tier" approach"*, by THELSEN, Manuel and SALZBERGER, Wolfgang.
- *"Voting in Europe: the Italian Case"*, by MICOSSI, Stefano and CHIAPPETA, Francesco.
- *"Evolving European Models: the Case of Spain"*, by TRIAS, Miguel.
- *"Governance – whose business is it?"*, by GILMOUR, Graham.
- *"Myths of Shareholders Value and Efficiency"*, LAZZARi, Walter.
- *"Clarifying the Roles of the Different Players"*, by DESCHAMPS, Marc.
- *"Governance at Troubled Companies"*, by CRAWFORD, Patricia Ayres.
- *"Final Report of the high Level Group of Company Law Experts"*, by Law Society, Comments submitted to the European Commission Company Law Committee (on Corporate Governance), February 2003.
- *"Impact of Independent Directors and the Regulatory Environment on Merger Prices and Motivation: Evidence from Large Bank Mergers in the 1990's"*, by BREWER III, Elijah, JACKSON III, William, JAGTIANI, Julopa, in Emerging Issues Series Supervision and Regulation Department Federal Reserve Bank of Chicago, December 2000.
- *"Is your Board fit for Challenge? Corporate Governance in Europe"*, by Heidrick & Struggles, Inc., 2003.
- *"Leading Corporate Governance Indicators, November 2002"*, by Davis Global Advisores, Inc., www.davis-global.com.
- *"O Governo das Sociedades Cotadas (Corporate Governance) em Espanha: - o Relatório Olivencia"*, by VELASCO SAN PEDRO, António, in BFD 75, 1999, pages 279-314.
- OECD Principles of Corporate Governance.
www.OECD.org/governance/principles.htm
- *"Principles of Auditor independence and Role of Corporate Governance in Monitoring and Auditor's Independence"*, by OICV-IOSCO, a Statement of the Technical Committee of the International Organisation of Securities Commissions, October 2002.

- *"Report on Matters of Corporate Governance Related to M&A Practice"*, by CAMEIRA, Maria Antónia, presented at the M&A Commission meeting, held during the annual UIA Congress 2002, Sidney, Australia.
- Review on the role and effectiveness of non-executive directors (Higgs Report), by HIGGS, Derek, January 2003.
www.ecgi.com
- *"Rights of Minority Shareholders"*, by CAMEIRA, Maria Antónia, in the International Corporate Law Bulletin (ICLB), Kluwer Publications, vol.2, Issue 3, March 1999.
- *"Statement on Global Corporate Governance Principles"*, Adopted 9th July of 1999, at the Annual Conference in Frankfurt.
- *"The Future of Corporate Governance in Europe Post-Enron"*, by European Corporate Governance Institute (ECGI), in www.ecgi.com
- *"The Globalisation of Corporate Governance"*, by DORE, Ron
www.ragm.com/library/topics/rondoreglobalisationofcorporategovernance21202.html
- *"Portuguese Ways of Improving Corporate Governance"*, by CAMEIRA, Maria Antónia, International Company and Commercial Law Review (ICCLR), London, England issue 12:10,October/2001
- *"The Role of Corporate Governance and Director's Liability in the Context of the Sale of a Business. Portuguese Report"*, by CAMEIRA, Maria Antónia, presented at the annual UIA Congress 2003, Lisbon, Portugal.
- *"Recent Developments regarding Corporate Governance: The Codes of Governance of Companies. Independence of Directors, Directors' Duties, Transparency, and Increasing Emphasis on the Rights and Role of Shareholders. The Winter Report. Portuguese Report"*, by CAMEIRA, Maria Antónia, presented at the annual UIA Congress 2003, Lisbon, Portugal.
- *"Rights of minority shareholders"*, by CAMEIRA, Maria Antónia, International Corporate Law Bulletin (ICLB), Kluwer Publications vol.2, Issue 3, March/1999,
- *"A Relação entre a Propriedade e a Gestão – Algumas Reflexões"*, by MATOS, Pedro Verga
- *"Commerce Bancshares, Inc. – Audit Committee Charter"*,
http://www.commercebank.com/027_audit.html
- *"Perspectivas de Convergência Global dos Sistemas de Direcção e Controlo da Sociedades"*, by EISENBERG, Melvin A., presented at the XXIV Annual Conference on the International Organization of Securities Commissions, 1999, Lisbon, Portugal,
http://www.cmvm.pt/estudos_documentos/documentos_em_arquivo/iosco99/eisenberg.asp

- *"Corporate Governance in Europe"*, European Shadow Financial Regulatory Committee, London, December 2002, http://www.ceps.be/2002/ESFRCCorpGov.pdf

- *"Strengthening Corporate Governance"*, *CrossCurrents* Winter 2002, by KROEGER, Barry F.,http://www.ey.com/global/content.nsf/US/Financial_Services_-_CC_-_Winter_2002_-_Strengthening_Corporate_Governance_-_P1

- *"What Lessons Can Be Learned from American and European Corporate Governance Scandals"*, by ARLMAN, Paul, presented at the Plenary Session III of the Foundation for European Corporate Governance, Brussels, November 2002
http://www.fese.be/initiatives/speeches/2002/fecg_brussels_29_november_2002.htm

- *"Corporate Governance in the Asian Financial Crisis"*, Transition Newsletter by JOHNSON, Simon, BOONE, Peter, BREACH, Alasdair and FRIEDMAN, Eric,
http://www.worldbank.org/transitionnewsletter/janfeb00/phs26-27.htm

- *"Dom Quixote or Robin Hood?: Minority Shareholder Rights and Corporate Governance in Korea"*, by LEE, Boong-Kyu, http://www.columbia.edu/cu/asiaweb/v15n2Lee.htm

- *"O Governo das Sociedades em Portugal: Uma Introdução"*, by CÂMARA, Paulo, Janeiro de 2001
http://www.cmvm.pt/legislacao_e_publicacoes/publicacoes/caderno12/gov_soc_port.pdf

- *"Sarbanes-Oxley: a Guide for Europeans"*, by DOOLEY, Daniel, in European Business Forum,
http://www.ebfonline.com/main_feat/trends/trends.asp?id=366

- *"Corporate Governance and Shareholder Returns"*, by FARRELL, Christopher,
http://www.nber.org/digest/dec01/w8449.html

- *"Draft Report of the Kumar Mangalam Birla Committee on Corporate Governance"*,
http://www.ecgi.org/codes/country_documents/india/corpgov.pdf

- *"A Corporate Governance Update"*, by KEANEY, Anne,
http://www.ethicalinvestor.com.au/columns/column.asp?Columnist_ID=23

- Autoridade Nacional de Comunicações (ANACOM)
http://www.anacom.pt

- Instituto de Seguros de Portugal (ISP)
http://www.isp.pt

- *"Código do Trabalho e Legislação Conexa – Anotados"*, by NETO, Abílio, September 2003, Ediforum – Edições Jurídicas, Lda

- Instituto dos Mercados de Obras Públicas e Particulares e do Imobiliário (IMOPPI)
http://www.imoppi.pt

- Banco de Portugal

 http://www.bportugal.pt/

- *"Enhancing Corporate Governance for Banking Organisations"*, Basel Committee on Banking Supervision, Basel, September 1999.

- *"Framework for the evaluation of internal control systems"*, Basel Committee on Banking Supervision, Basel, January 1998.

- *"The New Basel Capital Accord, Consultative Document"*, issued for comment by 31 July 2003, Basel Committee on Banking Supervision, April 2003.